A CHANCE AT CHILDHOOD AGAIN

A CHANCE AT CHILDHOOD AGAIN

Restoring Freedom and Wonder to Everyday Life

Alan D. Wright

MULTNOMAH PUBLISHERS

Sisters, Oregon

A CHANCE AT CHILDHOOD AGAIN
published by Multnomah Publishers, Inc.
© 1997 by Alan D. Wright

Cover photo by Hulton Getty/Tony Stone Images ©

International Standard Book Number: 1-57673-121-9
Printed in the United States of America

Unless otherwise indicated, Scripture quotations are from the *New
International Version* © 1973, 1984 by International Bible Society
used by permission of Zondervan Publishing House

For information:
MULTNOMAH PUBLISHERS, INC.
Post Office Box 1720
Sisters, Oregon 97759

Library of Congress Cataloging-in-Publication Data
Wright, Alan (Alan D.)
    A chance at childhood again/by Alan Wright.
        p.cm.
    Includes bibliographical references.
    ISBN 1-57673-121-9 (alk. paper)
    1. Faith. 2. Children--Religious life. 3. Wright, Alan (Alan D.)
I. Title.
BT771.2.W75   1997
248.8'4--dc21   97-10614
                                                            CIP

97 98 99 00 01 02 03 04 — 10 9 8 7 6 5 4 3 2 1

For Anne, my sparkling bride

Living with a princess makes even me feel like royalty.
Thanks for loving me these twelve years
and for being my best friend.
I wish I had lived next door to you as a kid.

Contents

Acknowledgments

Thanks to:

Bennett…for giving me "nose mashes" and bringing big doses of Heaven into our home. How strange, you want to be like me; but oh, how I want to be like you.

Mom…for telling me about your Father so I could be His child too. These pages are the product of the prayers you've prayed over me for years.

My families…Wrights, Wrens, Lynches, Curries, Budds. If you were the only people on earth, it would feel a lot like Heaven—but I'd still find a lot of illustrations in you.

Friends like…Lori Burhans, who thought I could write before I had written…Ray Cobb, who, if the whole world walked away, would still stand by me…Bill Dudley, I still can't believe how much you believed in me…Richard Moore, where would my life be if your life had not been yielded to God?

Two congregations…Mt. Bethel, my affection for you has not faded…Reynolda, I'm astounded by your love for God but equally convinced we will be astonished by God's plan for us.

Two faithful assistants…Claudia Steele, perhaps the most generous person alive…Linda Cooke, your smile alone makes it fun to come to work.

My editor, Dan Benson…for wanting wide-eyed child-like wonder and for wanting me to write about it.

My Multnomah partners…for welcoming me. You seem to love Jesus even more than good books.

A Chance at Childhood Again

"I tell you the truth, unless you change and become like little children, you will never enter the kingdom of heaven."

MATTHEW 18:3

Do you ever yearn to be a child again?

I sure do.

Life was slower and simpler then. My biggest financial burden was counting the money in the shoebox at the lemonade stand. My greatest fear was getting caught while trying to "kick the can."

But life wasn't just easier as a child—it was better.

The warm summer days in my North Carolina neighborhood were long. But they weren't long *enough*. Sometimes I pretended not to hear Mom shouting, "Alan, come home! Bedtime!" I hated that word "bedtime." Yuck! Bedtime meant the end of the day. It meant the end of shooting hoops at the Ryans' house even if I was almost "around the world." It meant I couldn't see my friends until the next day (except for the rare treat of camping out with buddies in the backyard). I hated bedtime. It was sort of like mealtime, an unwelcome intrusion into my childhood fun.

How different for most of us adults. We love to stop for big buffets in the middle of the day. And bedtime? It's no fiend interrupting our fun. Admit it—the pillow is more delicious than the buffet. The bed is a welcome old friend that invites us to rest and hide the pain of the day.

Something happens between childhood and adulthood that changes our mind-set from "I wish this day would never end" to "I'm glad this day is done."

In fact, a lot of things change for the worse as we grow up.

Consider work, for example. When our little boy was eighteen months old, I carried him in the backpack as I mowed the lawn one day. Upon finishing the laborious task, I shoved the heavy mower back into the garage, hoping not to see the dreaded machine again for at least a week.

Mopping the sweat from my brow, I panted, "Whew, I'm glad that's over." My boy, Bennett, on the other hand, wept and shouted, "More!" and tried to pull the lawn mower back out. I gave him an emphatic "No," but chuckled as a strange thought occurred to me. *My toddler would give anything for the privilege of taking on the chores that I hate to do!* Consider the toys most toddlers want: plastic vacuum cleaners, fire trucks, dolls that wet their diapers, pretend ovens, and plastic shovels. What's the real difference between digging a moat around a sandcastle at the beach and digging a trench for a drain at the construction site? Something happens between childhood and adulthood that makes work feel like work.

And what about the fun of learning? Do you remember the thrill of learning to read? I couldn't wait to read for two big reasons: I wanted to unlock the mysteries of street signs and sing all the words to hymns. But beyond the reward of reading the surgeon general's warning under the Marlborough man and singing all the verses of "Amazing Grace" was the sheer thrill of gaining new knowledge.

Every child celebrates learning. The love of learning turns babies into crawlers, crawlers into stumblers, and stumblers into walkers. Nothing stops children from learning. Hard floors and bruised knees don't defeat their crawling. And humiliating public tumbles don't hinder their learning to walk.

Adults, on the other hand, tend to try once...fail...and quit. When was the last time you tried your hand at a new hobby or sought a new skill? Something happens between childhood and adulthood that makes a Thursday night sitcom more desirable than a course in English literature at a local college.

And when did you last laugh? I don't mean a momentary chuckle at a funny joke. I mean a real guffaw. I mean the uproarious, buckled-over, breathless, begging-for-relief kind of laugh. I mean the uncontrolled belly laugh of a baby who's being tickled. What adult doesn't crave such uncluttered joy?

Even childhood's disorderly, tearful moments are, if we are honest, deeply attractive. My toddler's fists full of chocolate cake don't frustrate me nearly as much as my own lack of such childlike abandon. And wouldn't it be healing if we could weep freely when we are hurt? Just imagine the hope that would be fostered if we could cry out for help in times of trouble.

Joy. Freedom. Trust. Peace. Imagination. Celebration. Spontaneity. Creativity. Curiosity. Openness. Wonder. Everything that makes life wonderful comes so easily, so naturally, to children.

Don't miss the irony here. Children experience such joy in life, yet they possess so few of the things that adults crave. They have no money, no prestige, no sex life, no power. They have few possessions and even fewer choices. How content would you be if someone denied you your "adult rights" to own property, drive a car, dine in fine restaurants, and choose when to go to bed? But think about it for a moment—have those adult rights ever brought you happiness?

Maybe you're reading this book because life has not turned out the way you imagined. Your sunlit expectations of a happy Christian life have been replaced with an eclipse of disappointment. Read on. There is hope in these pages.

Perhaps you're looking for a "holy breeze" to fan your

flickering spiritual flame. Maybe you can speak the proper evangelical jargon. You may even have earned several spiritual medals—mission work, spiritual gifts, ordination—you name yours. But deep down, if you're really honest, you realize that something is missing.

Or maybe you're wondering, "What's a Christian's life really supposed to be like?"

That's what this book is about. Every thought in these pages finds root in Jesus' words: "I tell you the truth, unless you change and become like little children, you will never enter the kingdom of heaven" (Matthew 18:3).

These words of Jesus echo a common biblical refrain:

- "A little child will lead them" (Isaiah 11:6).
- "From the lips of children and infants you have ordained praise" (Matthew 21:16).
- "No one can see the kingdom of God unless he is born again" (John 3:3).
- "You have hidden these things from the wise and learned, and revealed them to little children" (Matthew 11:25).
- "Let the little children come to me, and do not hinder them, for the kingdom of heaven belongs to such as these" (Matthew 19:14).

Join me for a journey back through the years. Hear the silly laughter of happy childhood friends. Feel the innocent freedom of those unpretentious times. Allow yourself the luxury of unhurried thought. Relax and recall the best moments of your childhood.

But keep this in mind: The pages that follow hold more than cute stories about childhood. The simple metaphor of childlike faith plumbs profound spiritual truth. Jesus invites you to more than a stroll down memory lane—He is offering you complete transformation.

Don't miss it. Please believe it. Jesus is offering you a chance at childhood again.

CHAPTER ONE

A Giant Step Backward

Childlike Humility

"Whoever humbles himself like this child is the greatest in the kingdom of heaven."

MATTHEW 18:4

Do you remember forming a circle in the schoolyard for a game of dodge ball or Duck, Duck, Goose? The teacher had everyone hold hands. Then, to make the circle bigger, she said, "Everybody take a giant step backward." Strange, isn't it? Some things only get bigger when we move backward.

Becoming like a child again feels like taking a giant step backward. Let's face it—as children we craved adulthood. We just couldn't wait to be "big." Big people got to stay up late and eat all the cake they wanted. How thrilling it must be, we thought, to take charge of our own lives.

Jesus' invitation to experience childhood again might sound like a bizarre move in the wrong direction. Could it be possible that in order for our lives to get bigger, we must hold hands and take a giant step backward?

"Who is the greatest in the kingdom of heaven?" (Matthew 18:1).

The question betrays the disciples' pettiness, so we've been taught. Here are the unsophisticated Galilean fishermen crudely arguing for bragging rights, so we suppose. How dare they expose their pitiful, personal agendas by even asking the question! I always imagined Jesus sighing with frustration, shaking His head, and rolling His eyes at their stupidity.

But, the more I think about it, the more I believe that asking, "Who is the greatest in the kingdom of Heaven?" wasn't so bad after all. It wasn't a trivial question.

It's not like the disciples were asking Jesus whose mustache He liked best. They weren't asking who was the greatest in the world's eyes. They wanted to know who was the greatest in the Messiah's eyes. What's wrong with that? What's wrong with wanting to be the kind of person who embraces the fullness of God's kingdom?

By the way, we might reconsider our opinion of another incident for which we scorn the disciples: "Let one of us sit at your right and the other at your left in your glory" (Mark 10:37). What's so bad about James and John wanting to be close to Jesus?

Rereading the Gospel accounts, I hear no frustration in Jesus' response. Instead, He seems glad for this "teachable moment." Even in the Book of Mark, where we see the disciples silently embarrassed about their argument, Jesus fishes for their question by asking, "What were you arguing about?" (Mark 9:33). Jesus apparently wasn't disgusted with them for wondering who would be the greatest in God's kingdom. He seemed to *want* them to ask the question.

Maybe Jesus is waiting for you to ask the same question. Chances are, if you're reading this book, you've already asked it. Allow me to rephrase it: "What kind of person has the most heavenly life?"

Isn't that what all disciples of Jesus want to know? If your hungry heart has had so much as one tender taste of the Bread of Life, you crave more. If your parched soul has been whetted with even the smallest sip of Living Water, you thirst for deeper drafts.

Maybe the disciples asked the question because they had "[tasted] and [seen] that the LORD is good" (Psalm 34:8).

I don't aim to smooth over the disciples' rough spots. It's true—they were, on the whole, a bumbling band. And they probably tried Jesus' patience often. But when they debated the question of greatness in God's kingdom, they landed upon Jesus' favorite subject.

And so He taught them.

We always learn best by associating a new idea with an old, familiar one. The farmers of fertile Galilee could understand sowing the seed of the Word. Casters of nets could become fishers of souls. Keepers of flocks could follow a Good Shepherd. So the Master Rabbi seized the moment and taught as He always did, by example. "He called a little child and had him stand among them" (Matthew 18:2).

The Greek word suggests it was a small child. In a similar instance, Luke says that people were "bringing babies to Jesus" (Luke 18:15). Mark says that Jesus took a child, a boy, in His arms (Mark 9:36).

I wish I could have been there to see why the Messiah was so good with children. I wonder if the Creator took note of how soft a toddler's skin feels and squeezed the boy for fun. I wonder if the Holy One of Israel made a silly face to put the boy at ease.

Can you envision the sheepish grin that crept over this boy's face as he was put into the eternal spotlight? Imagine the shock of Jesus' astounding declaration: "Whoever humbles himself like this child is the greatest in the kingdom of heaven" (Matthew 18:4).

The disciples were certainly surprised at this odd answer. They probably murmured in disappointment. A child? Children were nothing in that culture. They had no rights. They were nobodies. Why, the disciples made it part of their job to keep the pesky little people away from Jesus! The King of Israel could not be bothered with such distractions.

What possibly could be so great about this little child? The lad probably couldn't even quote the Torah. He had no ministry skills. No education. No money. No power. This boy couldn't preach or teach. He probably had never fasted or given alms. How could he be great in the kingdom? What could a little child possibly know that the disciples didn't know?

At least one thing.

That little boy knew at least one thing that most adults aren't so sure of: The boy knew that he wasn't in charge of the world.

Every child knows that ultimately adults are in control. Adults say when it's bedtime. Adults set food on the table. And only adults have the right to answer, "Because I told you so." Oh sure, our persistent little people try to manipulate us in every way imaginable. But their defiance is only a test to see how far we'll let them go.

Deep down, every child knows that adults are bigger, stronger, and smarter. Children are not in charge of the world, and they know it.

That's their key to Heaven on earth.

They seldom go to bed at night worrying about what tomorrow holds. Some adult, a parent or teacher, will determine what tomorrow holds.

Children have no concept of dread. Your little girl may not even know she's going to the dentist until she gets there. (Aren't you glad?)

Children celebrate better because they don't have to be the best at everything. They enjoy another's accomplishment as much as their own.

Their lives are filled with wonder because they know they've seen only a small part of a very big world.

Their imaginations are glorious because they don't assume that if they've never seen it, it can't happen.

Their work is really play because they aren't worried about making a mistake and blowing their careers.

Adulthood is so difficult because we act like we're in charge of our own destiny. The role of "destiny maker" is a draining one. Though we pretend to be masters of our world, we secretly know ourselves to be impostors.

We know we're not properly equipped to be destiny makers. No matter how meticulous our DayTimers, we really don't have any idea what tomorrow holds. We can't determine the most basic conditions of life, such as the weather or our health.

I once served as a counselor for third-grade campers at a Christian camp in the North Carolina mountains. It was an especially hot, dry, Carolina July. On the way to arts and crafts, I overheard one of my campers say thoughtfully to another, "I sure hope it rains soon. My grandmother's garden needs water."

Immediately his friend let out a confident war cry and began a primitive rain dance. A third child then chimed in, "Don't be so silly. God's not going to make it rain just because of your stupid dance."

Now defiant, the original "rain wisher" made a grand theological statement: "God can do anything He wants to!"

The first step to childhood is the most important one. You must admit that God can do whatever He wants—and that you can't. It means accepting the fact that you are not in charge of the world, nor of your own life. You can't be a child and be in charge. You can't be a child if you are trying to be God.

I know you've worked very hard to get to where you are in life. The world taught you to take charge of your own destiny—it taught me that too. So it seems scary to let go of the little bit of control you feel you've obtained. It's hard to believe that life could be better with less control, less choices, and less power.

But remember your childhood. There was a time when you had so little, but had so much. And remember Jesus.

Your attitude should be the same as that of Christ Jesus:

> Who being in very nature God,
>> did not consider equality with God something to
>>> be grasped,
> but made himself nothing,
>> taking the very nature of a servant,
>> being made in human likeness.

And being found in appearance as a man,
>   he humbled himself
>   and became obedient to death—even
>   death on a cross!
>   (Philippians 2:5–9)

Children never grasp at equality with God. They know they're not in charge. God is waiting patiently for you to make that same, simple discovery.

Who is the greatest in the kingdom of Heaven? The one who humbles himself most. And who humbled Himself most? The One who came from the throne of Heaven to the cross on earth. Don't forget about Christmas! Jesus had firsthand knowledge about becoming a child.

If it feels scary to let go, remember Him. Born in a cave, bedded in a feeding trough, the Lord of Lords became a child. You can too. I know it sounds strange. But the best step you could ever take is one, giant step backward.

CHAPTER TWO

"More!"
Childlike Neediness

*To him who is able to do immeasurably more
than all we ask or imagine...*

EPHESIANS 3:20

I played halfback for the church peewee football team. And let me emphasize *wee*. Because of my wee size, I'm not sure I was the best halfback available. But my dad was the coach. Need I explain further?

Sometimes the peewee line blocked well. Occasionally, I made a good run. I even had a few moments of glory in the peewee end zone. But secretly, I knew my limitations.

Part of my job as halfback was to return punts and kicks. Most running backs look forward to kick returns because of the dynamic possibility of scampering down the field and dazzling opponents. But I didn't like kick returns. They didn't usually end in cheers. More often they ended in near-death experiences.

It was especially awful when we played the Police Club. They were anything but peewee. The Police Club

25

could have held its own against most NFL expansion teams. And worse, because the brutes scored touchdowns at will against my church team, the Police Club got lots of opportunities to kick the ball to us.

I would take my position to receive the kick alongside another running back. There I was. I looked like a kick receiver. I stood at the proper spot. I poised myself in the ready position. I awaited the kick.

Little did anyone know that I prayed, "O Lord, I beg Thee, do not let this ball come to me. Let it go out of bounds. Let it go to my teammate. But whatever You do, don't let it fall into my hands! And don't let me fall into the hands of the Police Club defenders."

Christians, take note. It is possible to look like a receiver while secretly hoping not to receive a thing. Every pastor has seen too much of this kind of attitude: prayers that aren't really prayers; couples who seek counseling but secretly don't want their marriages to heal; worshipers who expect nothing to happen. A lot of Christians talk about God providing. Few actually expect the provision. And when the ball's in the air, they aren't sure they want to catch it.

The main problem for most Christians is not giving— it's receiving.

I've never counseled a parishioner who was distraught over the inability to give. All the well-meaning Christians I know believe in giving (everything but money, but that's a different book). I've never had someone weep in my study and declare, "I just don't know if I'm willing to wash the dishes after Wonderful Wednesday dinner." Many *have* tearfully admitted, "I can't accept the fact that God loves me."

Adults have a problem receiving. Children don't. Getting stuff he or she wants is the toddler's main goal in life. An honest Sunday school department posted what they called "The Toddler's Creed."

> If I want it, it's mine.
> If I give it to you and change my mind later, it's
>   mine.
> If I can take it away from you, it's mine.
> If I had it a little while ago, it's mine.
> If it's mine, it will never belong to anyone else, no
>   matter what.
> If we are building something together, all the
>   pieces are mine.
> If it looks like mine, it's mine.
>
> (author unknown)

Toddlers are famous for trying to get stuff from others. They are sophisticated beggars and accomplished thieves. They will keep their arms outstretched toward anyone who has what they want. If they can take it from another toddler, they'll take it. If they can't get it, they'll make sure everyone else is as miserable as they are.

Toys, love, candy, hugs—you name it. If it's good, toddlers want somebody to give it to them.

Adults strive for the opposite outlook. We aim to be independent. We want to make it on our own. To ask for help is a sign of failure. To need no one's help is considered a triumph.

Men, what went through your mind the last time you were lost on a trip? Did you quickly look for someone to give you directions? Oh, you preferred using a map. Didn't have a map? You just drove around in circles until you found it on your own? I understand; after all, you've got a great sense of direction.

Women, what went through your mind the last time you wanted to lose a few pounds? Did you put it on the prayer list at church and join a weight-loss club for accountability? Oh, you'd rather try the *Buns of Steel* video in the privacy of your own home? I understand.

Somewhere along the path to adulthood, we become embarrassed to ask for help. We have a hard time receiving the most basic human needs like love, comfort, and affection.

I once interned in a large church with many caring people. The associate pastor for congregational care beamed as he explained the new lay-ministry course in congregational care. About a hundred saints had gone through weeks of intensive training in Christian caregiving and counseling.

These eager caregivers received a lot more training in pastoral care than most ministers do in seminary.

My minister friend glowed as he told me of the ministry's successful training sessions. But I could tell by his face something was missing in the new program.

"Why hasn't it worked?" I asked.

"Hardly anyone is willing to have a lay minister visit them," he admitted.

If you've ever tried to help people you love, you've probably heard the common refrains:

- "I don't want to put anyone out of his way."
- "I don't want to be a burden to my children."
- "I hate to bother my neighbors."

The world applauds independence. The Son of God grieved it: "How often I have longed to gather your children together, as a hen gathers her chicks under her wings, but you were not willing" (Matthew 23:37b).

How ironic! God is willing to give, but we are unwilling to receive.

Moms, would you really rather your teenage daughter cry alone in her bedroom than on your shoulder? Dads, would you really rather your little boy learn to hit a baseball by himself than with your instruction?

God the Father delights in helping you. He loves to rescue you, to inspire you, to teach you. He longs to hold you, to caress you, to tickle you, to rock you. God would prefer that you be like a pesky toddler rather than a self-sufficient adult. He'd even prefer that you whine a little with your arms outstretched rather than remain silent with your arms smugly folded.

In a parable on prayer, Jesus emphasized childlike persistence in asking for what is needed. An unexpected guest visited a friend whose cupboard was bare. There was only one way for the host to get what he needed: He asked a friend. When he didn't get the bread right away, he asked again—and again—and again. "I tell you, though he will not get up and give him the bread because he is his friend, yet because of the man's boldness [or persistence] he will get up and give him as much as he needs" (Luke 11:8).

What a strange principle Jesus was teaching! Listen to what Jesus was suggesting: "Nag, whine, plead, poke, prod—do whatever it takes to get what you need."

No need to teach toddlers this idea. They've already got it down pat.

Fathers don't have to teach their children to pull on Daddy's trousers repeatedly when they want something. Mothers don't have to teach babies how to cry for milk. No need to teach little ones how to stretch out their arms when they want to be held. Making requests comes quite naturally to little children. It's the only way they'll ever get what they want.

When the disciples asked Jesus how to pray, He gave

them a simple model. It boiled down to something like this: "Daddy, please give us the stuff we need." The Lord's Prayer (Matthew 6:9–13) is a series of requests:

- let Your name be holy
- send Your kingdom
- give us food for soul and body
- clean us up
- help us get rid of our grudges
- keep us from destroying ourselves in sin

The Lord's Prayer compares more closely to the "Toddler's Creed" than to our adult desire for self-sufficiency.

Jesus said, "Ask...seek...knock" (Matthew 7:7). That's what toddlers do best. And, as strange as it may seem, God likes to hear those requests.

I remember when our toddler, Bennett, learned the word *more*. I found it hard to resist. I admit I'm a sucker for anything cute. Smudged-faced grins and requests for more cake while there is still some in his mouth get to me. I'm prone to lose all parental rationality and say, "OK, just one more bite."

I know Christians should be suspicious of the word *more*. Just think of the Messiah who had no place to lay His head. Compare our sinful obsessions to have more of everything. We've seen the evil that arises in those whose greed creates an undying need for more power, more status, more popularity. Wars are fought and people are killed because of people's insatiable hunger for more.

And as adults, we understand scarcity. Resources are scarce. There *isn't* always more fuel, or more food, or more money available. We've all known times when things had to be divided and shared.

The last thing I want is to unwittingly teach my boy that there is always more available to him. I want him to learn contentment. I want him to learn sharing. I want him to learn to give with a glad heart. What a disservice it would be to spoil him rather than equip him for life! So I've wondered why it's so tough to say no to Bennett's requests for more. Then it occurred to me.

It has to do with the context in which he learned the word *more*. Anne and I taught him the word by necessity. No other word would do. We wanted to have some way of telling this little boy how much he means to us.

So I asked him, "Bennett, do you know how much your daddy loves you?"

He didn't answer.

It occurred to me that I had no answer either.

How can you put the infinite into time-trapped words? How can you give human terms to this love born in Heaven?

I decided to explain it in a way familiar to every parent. I stretched out my arms as wide as they would go. I asked him again, "How much does Daddy love Bennett?"

He regarded my silly pose with amusement. Stretching my arms even further, I declared, "I love you *more* than this!" Ever since, when I ask Bennett, "How much does Daddy love you?" he smiles and shouts, "*More!*"

I don't want my boy to lose that word from his vocabulary. I want him always to want more of his father's love. I want him to know that his father's love will never run out. I want him to know there will always be more.

When it comes to the blessing of God, you might as well learn to say "more." Your Heavenly Father's love never runs out. The riches of His grace are unsearchable and without end. And guess what? When you say "more," your Father has a tough time saying no. He loves you *more* than you can imagine.

> I pray that you, being rooted and established in love, may have power, together with all the saints, to grasp how wide and long and high and deep is the love of Christ, and to know this love that surpasses knowledge—that you may be filled to the measure of all the fullness of God.
>
> Now to him who is able to do immeasurably *more* than all we ask or imagine...be glory. (Ephesians 3:17–21)

There is only one word adequate to describe the Lord's love: *More.* I don't know the ways that you have experienced

His grace, but I know this: There is more. I can't say what you felt upon first seeing the love in Jesus' eyes. But this I can say for sure: There is more. I can't see the ways His glory glows in you. But I see this clearly: There is more.

How strange. He has more love to give than His people want to receive.

To become a child again, try this: Close your eyes, stretch your arms toward Heaven, and shout, "More, Father!" Why not ask God for every good thing He has to offer?

> "If you then, though you are evil, know how to give good gifts to your children, how much more will your Father in heaven give the Holy Spirit to those who ask him!" (Luke 11:13)

CHAPTER THREE

When Less Is More

Childlike Simplicity

"Seek first his kingdom and his righteousness,
and all these things will be given to you as well."

MATTHEW 6:33

"Daddy?"

"Yes," I responded to Bennett who was calling me from his car seat.

"Bennett—too little."

The very words were pitiful. And he said them pitifully. My wife and I glanced at one another in mild disbelief, not sure we heard our boy correctly.

"What did you say, sweetheart?"

He spoke the pitiful words again. "Bennett—too little."

Some tender spot in me got poked. I was the youngest of three boys. I was always the little one. The neighborhood kids affectionately called me "Lil' Al." When I finally bloomed, my flowering stopped at five feet eight and one-half inches. So I knew what it was like to be too little. Too little to stand up to the neighborhood bully. Too little to play on the basketball team. Too little even to think about asking a tall girl to the prom.

I never wanted to hear my boy say those words, "Too little." I never imagined he'd utter them before being two years of age.

Futilely we questioned him: "Why did you say that, Bennett?" But twenty-one-month-old children don't answer *why* questions. It turned out that he didn't need to answer after all. We figured it out.

My extended family, vacationing together at the beach, had piled into several cars and were headed to the rides. It was a historic evening for us. What parents can forget the first time they took their first child to the kiddie rides at the beach? Bennett had ridden the carousel at the mall. But this was different. He was going to the *real* amusement park where he would ride little cars and boats all by himself, and we would lean over the aluminum railings and smile and take pictures and wave and squeeze each other and say, "That's our little boy!" Bennett didn't know what a treat he was in for, but we could hardly wait.

It was on the way to the rides that he said, "Bennett— too little."

The real reason his three words got to us was that they were true. Evidently one of his older cousins, with no malicious intent, wanted to prepare Bennett for the fact that he wasn't big enough to ride some of the rides. In fact, when we arrived at the amusement park, we discovered that kids had to be at least two years old to ride anything, unless they were accompanied by a parent. A carousel and a little train were the only amusements he was technically allowed to go on by himself. A carousel and a train! He'd been on those before. My boy had come for power rides! So he flashed a "fake ID" and got on the little boats and the little cars that go around in an endless circle (but which all the toddlers are convinced they are steering).

As pitiful and heartrending as they were, Bennett's words were altogether true. Bennett was too little. Too little for the go-carts. Too little for the Himalayan ride. Too little for a Ferris wheel or roller coaster or that contraption that spins around until you get sick and then drops out its floor. Bennett was too little. There was no debating that. Though I sneaked him onto the little cars and boats, most of the rides had a height chart at the entrance. The signs said clearly, "You must be this tall in order to ride."

In fact, Bennett was not just too little for amusement-park rides. He was too little for almost everything. Toddlers have very few choices. That's why every kid wants to get big quick. Do you remember what it was like? It seemed like adults had everything, and as little children, we had nothing. Think about how few choices children get.

Compare the kids' menu to the adults' menu at most restaurants. While adults feast on a variety of gourmet cuisine, children choose between the grilled cheese, the hot dog, or the chicken fingers. But the limitations aren't confined to menus. Children get few choices in almost every arena.

Toddlers don't choose their own bath time or bedtime.

They don't set their own daily schedules.

They have little or no money.

They can't read. But if they could, they would be too little to get a library card.

They can't drive, so they can't choose where to go.

They're stuck with the friends who happen to live nearby or who are chosen by their parents.

When we were children, we craved the coming days of adulthood when we would have lots of choices. Adults love choices. Notice the success of restaurant buffets, huge superstores, and megachurches.

That's why adults love money too. Money gives us choices. The more we have, the more clothing fashions and real-estate markets we can choose from.

Not only do baby boomers love choices, they want to choose all the choices! I've directed a large renewal conference that features main speakers, worship, special musical concerts, seminars, and youth and children's ministries. Every year the main complaint is, "The weekend is too crowded." It never occurs to anyone that they don't have to attend all the meetings.

Some good friends made a pilgrimage to Disney World not long ago. Hearing them tell about it sounded more like a military campaign than a vacation. They had ordered maps of the theme parks well in advance for reconnaissance work. They strategized the best plan of attack, reviewing possible obstacles such as long lines and bad weather. Their mission: to do it all. Better yet: to do it all and bring back pictures to prove it.

The adults have all the choices. But who enjoys Disney World more—the adults or the little children?

Strange, isn't it? Little children have so few choices, but they have so much life. Their possessions and power are so scarce, yet their lives are so abundant. Could it be possible that fewer choices could add up to more life? How could less be more?

Consider this. Lion tamers sometimes enter a cage of lions with only a stool. They point the legs of the stool at the cats. What a flimsy defense against the king of the jungle! How can a lion tamer feel safe with only a stool pointed at the lion?

The four legs of the stool confuse the cat. Evidently, a lion cannot focus on more than one object at a time. Four chair legs approaching at the same time mentally immobilize the animal.

People have the same problem.

Imagine my announcing to you, "Your house is on fire!" "Your toddler is playing in the street!" "Your spouse has been put in jail!" "Your neck is bleeding!" What would you do? You could handle any one of the problems readily. But all four coming at the same time? It's enough to paralyze a person. Do you ever have days when there's so much to do that you do nothing?

It doesn't have to be problems that paralyze us. Simultaneous triumphs can be debilitating as well. "You just had a baby girl!" "The Publisher's Clearing House is at your door!" "Your boss called; you got the promotion!" "The drillers just struck oil in your yard!"

Efficient managers may learn to multitask. Emergency rooms practice triage. But the human soul was designed to have one focus. The heart divided with complex loyalties is never content. The heart that keeps one simple focus enjoys freedom.

Jesus taught this profound truth when He said, "Seek first his kingdom and his righteousness, and all these things will be given to you as well" (Matthew 6:33). It's one simple choice: His kingdom. It's an eternal promise: Less means more. Give up other choices for this one, and your blessings will be far greater than those people's who choose it all.

Eleven years ago my bride seemed to float down the aisle toward me. My nerves were overtaken by the wonder and beauty of the moment. I saw past the sparkle and looked deeply in her eyes as I spoke the words, "I, Alan, take you, Anne…." Thoughts such as, "Alan, do you realize what you are giving up?" and "What about all the other women in the world?" never crossed my mind. Instead, my soul felt the pleasure of God as I made a simple vow.

One choice among many. I've never once doubted the choice or even been tempted to waver from it, for my wife is my single greatest earthly delight. Marriage means choosing one person. It means blatantly ignoring all other choices.

I've known many blissfully wedded couples. I've never met a promiscuous person whose soul was satisfied. I've never known an adulterer who was fulfilled.

If you try to grab hold of everything, you'll lose it all. But if you hold on to the single most important thing, you'll have all you need.

Let your soul have one simple aim. Let God have your whole heart. His Word repeats this refrain again and again.

• "Hear, O Israel: The LORD our God, the LORD is one. Love the LORD your God with all your heart and with all your soul and with all your strength" (Deuteronomy 6:4–5).

• "Trust in the LORD with all your heart and lean not on your own understanding; in all your ways acknowledge him, and he will make your paths straight" (Proverbs 3:5–6).

• "You will seek me and find me when you seek me with all your heart" (Jeremiah 29:13).

• "Jesus replied: 'Love the Lord your God with all your heart and with all your soul and with all your mind. This is the first and greatest commandment'" (Matthew 22:37–38).

Don't confuse simplicity with the absence of belongings. Jesus isn't nearly as concerned with what you *have* as with what you *seek*. All of our attics and garages could probably use a good cleaning. But Jesus is not concerned primarily with cluttered closets. He cares about cluttered souls.

In His invitation to experience childhood again, Jesus doesn't offer you more choices. He offers less choices. Children have so few choices, but have so much life. Isn't it time to let your soul settle on one central priority?

It may sound strange, but in God's way of thinking, less is more. Less loyalties mean more devotion to Him. Fewer choices magnify the one choice—Jesus.

CHAPTER FOUR

"Uh-Oh"
Childlike Failure

"Lord, if it's you...tell me to come to you on the water."

MATTHEW 14:28

My family made memories at Myrtle Beach, South Carolina. The same week every summer the Driftwood became our paradise. Just the mention of that simple oceanfront motel puts my mind adrift in the sea of sweet recollections. The hearty laugh of Jake, the waiter in the Driftwood restaurant...the blended aroma of the sea breeze across tropical shrubs on the grounds...the scratch of my father's unshaven face against mine when he held me in the waves...sandcastles...and, of course, Skee Ball.

The Driftwood, you see, had several distinct geographical advantages over lesser accommodations: (1) It was a short walk to the ocean; (2) It was a short walk to the foot-long hot-dog stand; (3) It was a short walk to the arcade. Oceans and foot-long hot dogs haven't changed

43

that much over the years, but arcades sure have.

That particular Myrtle Beach gameroom was not filled with the lights and sounds of Mortal Combat video games but with the clack, thump, and roll of Skee Balls. You've probably seen this ancient game in which brown, wooden balls are rolled up a ramp toward holes in ascending circles with point values increasing from ten to fifty. Today, if you can find a Skee Ball game, a perfect score will net you about five coupons. Once you've spent about ten dollars worth of quarters and accumulated two hundred coupons, you can redeem them for a small stuffed animal worth around fifty cents.

But in my Driftwood days, Skee Ball was only a dime, and a score of 340 won a fairly plump teddy bear. Winning was unusual, but not impossible, for a youngster. Those bears could be had. And we wanted to have them. As additional incentive, we knew that ordinary towns were not blessed with Skee Ball arcades in those days. The Myrtle Beach pavilion was the only one we'd see all year. So my brothers and I became serious Skee Ball players.

If adult athletes would approach their sport with the determination of a child at a Skee Ball ramp, every neighborhood would have Olympians. The remarkable accomplishment of our Skee Ball playing days was not how often we won (the stuffed animals were few and far between). The remarkable thing was how often we lost, without quitting. It never crossed our little minds that just because we'd failed dozens of times that we'd fail next time also. The stuffed animal was only one more dime, one more fifty-point roll away from being ours.

My middle brother, Mark, had particular determination. I think it was because he was stuck between my eldest brother, David, who seemed to win at everything quite effortlessly, and me, the baby, who won less but managed to be cute while losing. Anyway, Mark has always possessed prizefighter tenacity.

One summer on our first day at the Driftwood, David promptly won a stuffed animal. Seeing how easily the bear was won, Mark determined in his heart to win on the first day of vacation as well. With his winning resolve, little Mark spilled open his entire piggy bank, and with his life's savings in hand, he marched to the arcade.

He didn't win.

I don't know how many times he played Skee Ball that day. I don't know how many dimes he slipped into that slot. The amount didn't matter. What mattered was that it was all he had. And he hadn't won.

That little boy had to walk back to the Driftwood with no stuffed bear and no dimes. He brought only his tears. You might imagine why he was crying. His money was gone the first day. It wasn't really his life's savings, but it was his whole allowance for the beach trip. It meant there was no money left for T-shirts or toys from the Gay Dolphin Gift Cove. It meant no Swamp Fox roller coaster

or wild Himalayan ride. There was no money left for foot-
long hot dogs or saltwater taffy.

But I don't think those material losses were the source
of his grief.

He grieved not for the loss of coins nor the absence of
prizes. Instead, he wept at the prospect of no more Skee
Ball. No more chances to perfect the flick of his wrist. No
more chances to win. Don't be confused. Little Mark was
no gambler addicted to a game of chance. Skee Ball is all
skill. Surely, if he had one more dime, he could win.

Later in life, organized sports would teach us a lot
about winning, losing, and never giving up. But it was
there, in the Skee Ball arcade, that we learned some of our
earliest lessons about the thrill of victory and the agony of
defeat.

I still secretly long for the Skee Ball arcade of thirty
years ago. But I yearn even more for the heart of the child
who played the game. I don't advise spending your life's
savings on Skee Ball, but I do invite you to consider the
invincible spirit of childhood that refuses to be crushed by
a little losing. The spiritual lesson from Skee Ball, and from
childhood, is not in how to win, but in how to fail.

Failing is what little children do best. That is to say,
little children fail a lot but seldom feel like failures. Adults,
who fail far less, tend to feel like failures.

How many times would you be willing to spit up on
yourself in public before giving up on warm milk?

How many times would you be willing to strain the muscles in your entire body just for the chance of rolling over?

How many times would you be willing to fall on your bottom in front of cheering onlookers just for the chance to walk?

How many times would you let the asphalt skin your knee just for the chance to conquer a bike without training wheels?

Children fail a lot at a lot of things. And, most of the time, their failure is public. Conversely, one good public failure is enough to send many adults into seclusion. Such a retreat would never occur to small children. They know that goofing up goes with the territory of being a little kid.

Besides, toddlers never consider failure to be final. Can you imagine a crawler falling on his first attempt at toddling and declaring, "Well, that's it. I guess I was never meant to walk"? Can you imagine a three-year-old accidentally wetting her bed once and deciding therefore to wear diapers for the rest of her life?

Little children never focus on their failures; they focus on their goals. Adults, on the other hand, become so consumed with their failures that they forget their goals.

Remember Peter's walk on the water? He began with the unconcerned impetuosity of a child: "Lord, if it's you...tell me to come to you on the water." For that moment, childlike Peter had no thought of failure. No thought of the wind or the waves or the darkness.

That's the way a child thinks. "If you can drive a car, Mommy, why can't I? Let me steer, Mom, let me steer!" There's no thought of running off the road or hitting trees or paying insurance bills. No thought of the potential failure—just the potential success.

Peter had no thought of sinking. He thought only of walking on water like Jesus: "Let me try that, Jesus! Let me try that!"

You might have expected a reasonable Messiah to reject such a childlike request. "Peter, foolish Peter," Jesus might have said. "Don't be ridiculous. You can't walk on water. You aren't nearly holy enough. I am God in the flesh. You are quite ordinary. Leave the water walking to me. What's the point of your walking to me anyway? What will it prove? Besides, look at this wind and these waves. Even if you could walk on water, this storm would swallow you up."

Instead, I think the Lord smiled when He said, "Come."

That one-word invitation was all it took. Peter went overboard.

The disciple looked at Jesus and walked on water. Then he looked at the wind and sank like a rock. He started out so like a child would. He finished so like an adult. He began with no thought of failure. He ended with nothing but failure on his mind. He started with childlike eyes on a prize. He ended with adult thinking about sinking. "But when he saw the wind, he was afraid and, [began] to sink" (Matthew 14:30). As soon as he focused on failing...glub, glub, glub.

Even then, Jesus did not scorn Peter's impulsive decision to try the impossible. There was no "I-knew-you-shouldn't-have-tried-it" rebuke. Instead, the Savior offered a hand of mercy and an invitation to trust more next time.

Peter was always prone to goof-ups. He was singled out as one of the disciples who couldn't keep his head up for one hour while Jesus was sweating blood in Gethsemane. Peter impulsively claimed that he would never deny his Lord, then failed Jesus three times before the cock crowed. In impetuous defense of Jesus, Peter was the disciple who excised the ear of the high priest's servant with a sword. Jesus followed Peter's blunder by giving the servant a new ear.

Peter, more than any other disciple, was prone to major mistakes. Jesus called him "dull" on one occasion (Matthew 15:16) and on another accused him of being a "stumbling block" and an agent of Satan (Matthew 16:23). But the Lord also declared that Peter would be the "rock" upon which He would build His church (Matthew 16:18).

Why did Jesus choose this sinking, slicing, denying disciple as His rock? Peter had blundered more than the rest of the disciples combined. This impetuous, impulsive, failure—the rock of the church?

Commentators vary on the interpretation of the passage. The Roman church says the rock is Peter himself, while some say the rock actually refers to Jesus. Others argue that the rock is the confession of faith.

Choose your doctrine, but don't miss the point of it all. Jesus was absolutely delighted with Peter's confession of Christ's Lordship and blessed him mightily:

> "Blessed are you, Simon son of Jonah, for this was not revealed to you by man, but by my Father in heaven. And I tell you that you are Peter and on this rock I will build my church, and the gates of Hades will not overcome it. I will give you the keys of the kingdom of heaven; whatever you bind on earth will be bound in heaven, and whatever you loose on earth will be loosed in heaven." (Matthew 16:17–19)

I'm sure Jesus was delighted with Peter's knowledge of His Messiahship. But He was more delighted to hear Peter acknowledge it out loud. The other disciples could not have been ignorant of Jesus' Lordship. They had been with this Messiah long enough to know that He was altogether different from John the Baptist and Elijah. But only Peter dared say it. While the others remained quiet, fearful of offering the wrong answer, Peter blurted it out from his heart. So Jesus blessed him.

Jesus would build His church not on the quiet reserve of cautious contemplators. Christ would build His church on men like Peter who would dare to preach the gospel out loud to a pagan world. Jesus would build His church on a few bold men who would not only risk failing but would be willing to give up all for the sake of winning the world for Christ. The gates of hell cannot overcome men or women who are willing to step out of the boat with their eyes on the prize. The Christian who is not afraid of failing cannot fail.

The Lord never once asked you to be without failure. But on every page of the Bible, He has asked you to be without fear. It is an unbroken biblical refrain: *Fear not, for I am with you.*

You'll never lead a single person to Christ if you're not willing to have plenty of people roll their eyes at you in disgust.

Strange, isn't it? You need to learn to fail if you are ever going to succeed.

My brother Mark was about six when he failed well. My parishioner Martha was about eighty-six. But she was every bit as much a child in spirit as was my Skee Balling sibling. And she was just as certain that one day she would win her prize.

Based on a brief look at her life, you might pity this

parishioner if you didn't know better.

First husband—abusive, abandoned her.

Second husband—died a slow death.

Her son—killed by cancer.

Her daughter—almost killed by a car.

But if you met Martha, you wouldn't pity her; you'd want to be like her. No amount of failures could ever make Martha feel like a failure. In fact, the more life failed her, the more determined she was to succeed.

She started a Bible study for seniors in her home. I agreed to teach the Gospel of John. The group started with about eight faithful participants. It ended with about four. On a few occasions, just Martha and I showed up. But still, Martha was always concerned about her apartment being too small to accommodate the group. Convinced it would grow to dynamic proportions, Martha had plans to move the study to the church fellowship hall.

One evening, Martha made a strange phone call to my wife. "I have some very good news. But you must promise not to tell a single soul other than your husband," she insisted.

"Of course I won't tell. What is it, Martha?" Anne asked.

"Well, you mustn't tell anyone. But I've won the sweepstakes."

"Martha! How? When? How much?"

"I don't know the amount yet. But I think it will be at

least one million dollars. They will deliver the check to my door soon. I also have an invitation to go to New York with other winners. By the way," she added, "I do plan to give a tithe to the church building fund."

When I called Martha to hear the joyous news for myself, I asked, "Martha, how are you certain you've won? Did a sweepstakes representative call you?"

"No. No one has called and actually said I've won," she confided. "I just keep getting these nice letters. I must have won—otherwise, why would they keep sending me these letters?"

Gulp.

I have seen those "nice letters." You have too. They are form letters that announce at the top, "Congratulations, Mr. John Doe. You are approved to win $1,000,000." Most people throw them away. Martha had responded to all of them.

I asked her if I could come take a look at the letters. I saw them. Ordinary form letters designed to prey on people like Martha. They sure made it sound like Martha had won. But the fine print was clear enough. Martha had won nothing.

I've groped for words to confront a beloved church leader about sin in his life. I've searched for words to comfort a mother whose son was just murdered. I've had plenty of difficult moments in ministry. But I don't remember anything tougher than lifting my eyes from those sweepstakes form letters, looking into her precious, eighty-six-year-old face, and announcing, "Martha, I don't think you've won."

I figured she'd be devastated.

Instead, she invited Anne and me for coffee and doughnuts the next Thursday morning—the date she expected the sweepstakes van to show up with her check. When we knocked on her door a little after the appointed time, Martha opened it with a smile. Behind her were some friends pointing a video camera at us.

"It's only us," we said. "Don't reckon you've heard anything?"

She hadn't. She never did.

In fact, Martha got sick the next year and, suddenly, was gone. In preparing her funeral service, I read Paul's words to the Romans:

> And we rejoice in the hope of the glory of God. Not only so, but we also rejoice in our sufferings, because we know that suffering produces perseverance; perseverance, character; and character, hope. And hope does not disappoint us, because God has poured out his love into our hearts by the Holy Spirit, whom he has given us. (Romans 5:2–5)

As I meditated on those words and thought of Martha's life, the Lord whispered to me a secret: "Alan, do you remember how Martha always thought she was going to win big? Now she has!"

Martha got the last laugh. She was no gullible widow living a fantasy. She *was* on the verge of striking it rich. She just had a couple of the details wrong. She didn't get a prize van and check at her apartment door. She got a chariot of angels and a ticket to eternity. She won unspeakable heavenly riches and moved into a mansion of glory.

Little children keep trying because they are certain they will eventually succeed. If you are a Christian, feel free to fail many times, because in the end, you will win big. We are "heirs of God and co-heirs with Christ" (Romans 8:17). No failure, no personal setback, no careless mistake, no idiotic blunder, no bad marriage, no ugly sin, no stupid investment, no failed exam, no lost promotion, no professional malpractice shall separate you from the love of God that is in Christ Jesus.

So go ahead. Roll another Skee Ball. Step out of the boat. Send in your sweepstakes ticket. Feel free to fail as much as you'd like. No number of failures can ever make you a failure. If you are a child of the Father, you're going to win big.

CHAPTER FIVE

"Who Am I?"
Childlike Identity

"I blessed him—and indeed he will be blessed!"

GENESIS 27:33

Bennett got a set of golf clubs for his second birthday. The small aluminum clubs were just his size, and they look like the real thing. They even came in their own wee golf bag with its own strap, golf tees, and plastic golf balls. Bennett could whack the ball pretty well after several tries. He could whack furniture well on the first try. Jack Nicklaus could not be prouder of his personally endorsed, multimillion-dollar golf club line than Bennett is of his tiny clubs in their plaid bag. When he is not swinging them, he likes just to hold them. He wants the clubs to travel wedged in his car seat. He would sleep with them if we let him.

A few days after his birthday, this little boy with a golf bag on his shoulder strode proudly into my study and announced, "Daddy, I'm a great golfer boy."

Where in the world did he get that idea?

OK, I admit it. I've talked to him about golf a little. And, yes, he might have seen me putting around the house occasionally. And, OK, he might have caught a glimpse of golf on TV some late Sunday afternoon. And, I must confess, there is the golfer-boy song.

We sing a lot in our house. We mainly sing a variety of praise songs. But Bennett sometimes requests personal ballads. He wants to hear songs about how Pooh Bear and Eeyore played with Bennett and how Barney found them in the Hundred Acre Wood. One day Bennett pleaded, "Sing a golf-ball song."

Ever since, whenever he makes that request, I sing a silly ditty about Bennett and Winnie the Pooh playing golf. In the song, Bennett is the first one on the tee and the refrain says,

> He hit the ball high
> Way up in the sky.
> It went so far, everyone waved bye.
> It sailed by the clouds.
> It flew past the sun.
> It landed on the green and made a hole in one!

It's clear. Bennett didn't just decide on his own that he was a golfer. He simply believed what his daddy told him. That's how all of us develop our identity.

You didn't just decide to be who you are. You believed what someone told you about yourself. It started while you were still in the womb. You were listening. You sensed how your mother felt about you as she carried you for nine months. And every day since your birth, you've been listening to what others say about you. You've been listening to find out who you are.

My wife studied early childhood development. My only contribution to her education was helping her cut out pictures from magazines for a large collage she once made for a class assignment. It was a bulletin board decoration consisting of pictures of children involved in various activities. Across the bottom of the display she stenciled in bold letters, "Who Am I?"

I secretly wondered about the merit of the work. There was no scholarly research accompanying it. No fancy essay attached. I silently wondered if the professor would respond favorably.

The assignment earned an A-plus and glowing remarks from her professor. "You have identified the most important question for any child's development," the professor commented. "Every child is asking that very question: 'Who am I?' Children are searching, every day of their little lives, for the answer to that—life's simplest, most profound question."

"Who am I?"

We don't find the answer from within. We find it outside

ourselves. We don't tell ourselves who we are. We take someone else's word for it.

For example, who decided on your name? You didn't. You couldn't have. They needed something to put on the birth certificate, and you couldn't talk. Your parents might have given careful thought to the meaning of your name. Or they might have picked it off a billboard. You may not particularly like it. But it's your name because it's what the most important people in your life decided to call you.

Think how strange it would be to have another name. Pick a different name for yourself and say it out loud. "Hi, I'm Sam Snodfelter." Try it. Call yourself some other name out loud. It's just not you, is it? You accepted the fact that you are who your parents named you.

Actually, you learned every facet of your identity from someone else. Whether you are a PGA champion or a world-class pianist, you believed somebody's affirmation of your ability. If you feel precious, it's because you believed someone who treasured you. If you feel worthless, it's because you believed somebody's abuse.

It's hard for us strong-willed, self-starting, independent, twentieth-century Americans to believe that someone else's words can determine our course. But every Old Testament Hebrew child knew it as fact. The whole path of a Hebrew boy's life depended on his father's blessing. The spoken word of the Hebrew father was not only mighty, it was irrevocable. One red-haired twin boy felt the full pang of this potent truth.

Esau was the first of Isaac and Rebekah's twins to emerge into the world. That simple fact entitled him to all the privileges of a firstborn son. The firstborn son in a Hebrew family was entitled to a double allotment of his father's inheritance. Though Jacob followed closely behind, holding on to his brother's heel, Esau would live his whole life anticipating a special measure of his dad's blessing.

But Jacob devised a cruel trick to steal his older brother's rightful blessing. The shocking story is recorded in Genesis 27.

"Isaac said [to Esau], 'I am now an old man and don't know the day of my death.... Prepare me...food I like and bring it to me to eat, so that I may give you my blessing before I die" (vv. 2, 4).

But while Esau left to hunt the game, Jacob and his mother conspired to fool the aged, blind father. "Then Rebekah took the best clothes of Esau her older son, which she had in the house, and put them on her younger son Jacob. She also covered his hands and the smooth part of his neck with the goatskins. Then she handed to her son Jacob the tasty food and the bread she had made" (vv. 15–17).

The dastardly conspiracy continued as Jacob appeared before his father and lied. "I am Esau your firstborn. I have done as you told me. Please sit up and eat some of my game so that you may give me your blessing" (v. 19).

At first, the elderly father questioned whether it was really Esau before him. But after smelling the clothes of his firstborn on Jacob, Isaac became convinced that it was Esau. With that confidence, the father spoke his blessing upon his thieving son: "May God give you of heaven's dew and of earth's richness—an abundance of grain and new wine. May nations serve you and peoples bow down to you. Be lord over your brothers, and may the sons of your mother bow down to you. May those who curse you be cursed and those who bless you be blessed" (vv. 28–29).

Moments later, Esau presented himself and his food to Isaac. Notice the horrified tremor in the father: "Isaac trembled violently and said, 'Who was it, then, that hunted game and brought it to me? I ate it just before you came and I blessed him" (v. 33).

Why the trembling? Why the horrified shock? All the father had done was speak a few words. Just words. Couldn't Isaac take them back? "Oops, I was fooled. I didn't mean what I said because I was deceived." Any court of law would restore the blessing back to Esau, the rightful recipient.

But Isaac was horrified because he knew a father's blessing to be irrevocable. "I blessed him—and indeed he will be blessed!" (v. 33).

The power of a father's words. The full, potent sting fell upon Esau: "When Esau heard his father's words, he burst out with a loud and bitter cry and said to his father, 'Bless me—me too, my father!'" (v. 34).

"Isaac answered Esau, 'I have made him lord over you and have made all his relatives his servants, and I have sustained him with grain and new wine.'" As Esau wept aloud, Isaac's words smothered him: "Your dwelling will be away from the earth's richness, away from the dew of heaven above. You will live by the sword and you will serve your brother. But when you grow restless, you will throw his yoke from off your neck" (vv. 37, 39–40).

The tongue, James says, is like the tiny rudder that steers a mighty ship or the spark that ignites a great forest fire. Words spoken with authority exert awesome, far-reaching power. If the neighborhood bully tells a child that she's ugly, it will hurt her feelings. If the father tells his child she's ugly, she will not only believe it, but she will *feel* ugly. And she probably will do everything she can to *look* ugly. In fact, she will believe it until someone more important tells her otherwise.

But imagine that one day the cursed daughter meets a much sought-after bachelor. He looks beneath the surface of homely insecurity that has shrouded the beauty of the young woman for years, and he sees a hidden treasure. Imagine how that young man courts that young woman with roses and poems and romantic dinners. And, over and over, he tells his beloved, "You are the most beautiful woman in the world."

She is confused and has a hard time believing her suitor. After all, the most important male figure in her life had told her she was ugly and would be lucky ever to find a husband. But slowly, as her love grows and her trust increases, she begins to accept the praise of her beau.

One day, the young man bows his knee, presents a sparkling diamond, and asks the young woman for her hand in marriage. On their wedding night, the husband looks into the eyes of his new bride and tells her again, "You are the most beautiful woman in the world." Now, having committed her life to him, knowing him to be the most important person in her life, she believes him. And the moment that she believes his praise she receives the blessing. From that moment on, she *is* a beautiful woman because the one who matters most has said so.

So who are you?

The answer to that question depends on whose words you believe. And that depends on who is the final authority in your life. You may have parents who called you stupid. But they are not the final authority in your life. You may have a husband who calls you a burden. But he is not the final authority in your life. You may have a wife who calls you a failure. But she is not the final authority in your life.

When Jesus offers you a chance at childhood again, He is inviting you to a whole new identity based on the words of a whole new authority. Jesus is inviting you to forget what everyone else has said about you and to believe what your Heavenly Father has declared.

The story recounted in Genesis 27 is a horrid, shocking tale. There isn't even a hint of fairness in it. Jacob was a conniving, lying thief who did not deserve his father's reward. Esau was an honest, hardworking lad duly entitled to his father's full blessing. Whatever sense of justice we possess cries out, "Lord, how can this be? How could you allow the blessing due this firstborn to fall upon the one who deserves it less?"

And when you ask that unanswerable question, you hit upon the inexplicable mystery of the gospel.

Eighteen hundred years after Isaac offered his blessing to the wrong child, another father did likewise. But this time, it was no mistake.

God's Son came to earth. He was the Father's only Son. His firstborn Son. And the Father's love for His Firstborn was great. Never once did Jesus make a mistake. Never once did He stray from His Father's will. He was without sin. He was perfect in every way.

Jesus, more than anyone who ever lived, deserved the full blessing of His Father. He deserved only Heaven's dew, earthly riches, and abundance of new wine. He deserved only the most sublime praise of His Father.

But instead, at the pinnacle of His ministry, a horrible, inexplicable reversal occurred. Instead of receiving His just reward, the sinless Firstborn was put on a cross to bear the curse of sin. The Son's agony was tremendous, His cry more bitter than Esau's: "My God, my God, why have you forsaken me?" (Mark 15:34). But the Father did not lift the curse. Instead, the Firstborn was mocked. His naked, destitute body was laid in a tomb.

In those same moments, the Father did the unthinkable. He took His hands of blessing off His Firstborn and stretched them toward you and me. He turned the sweet sound of His voice away from the deserving One and toward the ugly, conniving, lying younger siblings and offered them the blessing they did not deserve.

And so your Heavenly Father's blessing falls upon you. He has blessed you "with every spiritual blessing in Christ" (Ephesians 1:3). He called you Jesus' brother (Hebrews 2:11), and He looked upon you as His Firstborn, "holy in his sight, without blemish and free from accusation" (Colossians 1:22). He has made you His heir (Romans 8:17), declared you royalty, and ordained you a priest (1 Peter 2:9). He announced that He was for you and has forbidden anyone to stand against you (Romans 8:31), and He declared you "more than [a] conqueror" (Romans 8:37).

None of us deserves it. But once this blessing is spoken over you, it is final. He paid for it with an infinite price, and so He meant it for eternity.

If two-year-old Bennett believes he's a "great golfer boy" just because his daddy gave him a set of miniature clubs and sang him a song, how much more should you believe your Heavenly Father who gave you His Spirit and called you a saint? If anyone asks you who you are, tell them what your Father has said about you. And if you ever forget your identity, ask your Father; He would love to refresh your memory.

CHAPTER SIX

"But You Promised!"
Childlike Trust

"If you, then, though you are evil, know how to give good gifts to your children, how much more will your Father in heaven give good gifts to those who ask him!"

MATTHEW 7:11

In the precious months preceding our firstborn's birth, my expectant wife asked me, "Alan, what part of parenting excites you most? When you think of becoming a dad, what do you look forward to most?"

"Trust," I responded. "I look forward to having someone trust me in the way that little children trust their parents—so purely, so implicitly."

• "I look forward to feeling the full weight of a baby's body resting in my arms, knowing that if my arms give way, so does the baby."

• "I look forward to hearing our baby's cry disappear just because he smells me and I rock him quietly."

• "I look forward to the first time he lets me hoist him onto my shoulders for a walk."

• "I look forward to the rush of excitement on our toddler's face when he first jumps from the swimming pool's edge into my waiting arms—just because he trusts me."

• "I look forward to speaking to him and having him believe me completely."

"It may sound selfish at first, like an ego trip," I tried to explain to Anne. "But I really don't mean it that way. What I mean is that I look forward to having someone believe in me so fully that I can instill the confidence of Christ in him. I look forward to the window of pure trust that enables a father to shape the life of his child. My heart pounds with joy and excitement to know that our child will trust me so much that when I say, 'Jesus loves you,' he will believe it without hesitation. I can't wait to tell him that he can do all things through Christ who strengthens him, and watch that truth sink into his soul. Oh, how I look forward to that precious period of time when, though I don't deserve it, our child will, by design and by necessity, trust me totally."

Doesn't your Heavenly Father feel that way toward you?

When Jesus said, "Unless you change and become like little children, you will never enter the kingdom of heaven" (Matthew 18:3), maybe it was because He had asked His Father the same question Anne had asked me. Maybe on the sixth day of Creation when the Father said, "Let us make man in our image" (Genesis 1:26), Jesus interrupted Him and said, "Father, before You speak the word, let Me ask You a question: 'What excites You most about creating these creatures in Your own image?'"

Maybe the Father paused long enough to respond:

• "I look forward to breathing life into them and knowing that if I quit breathing, so will they."

• "I look forward to seeing Noah's family pile into the ark before the sight of the first rain cloud."

• "I look forward to seeing Abram's smiling face lift toward the night sky when I tell him how many descendants he will have."

• "I look forward to Moses' staring down the Egyptian army without fear before I even start rolling back the Red Sea's waters."

• "I look forward to Your garden prayer, Son, when You will say, 'Not my will' just because You still trust My plan."

Trust. It's what God loves most in us. You can hardly find a page of His Word in which He doesn't ask for it:

• "Trust in the LORD with all your heart and lean not on your own understanding" (Proverbs 3:5).

• "Trust in the LORD forever, for the LORD, the LORD is the Rock eternal" (Isaiah 26:4).

• "Do not let your hearts be troubled. Trust in God; trust also in me" (John 14:1).

We were made to trust Him. He painted trust with every brush stroke in the masterpiece of human creation. Trust is the foundation and building block by which He sketched the blueprints. Trust is the refrain of the song between earth and Heaven. The Lord wants our trust so passionately. Why do we have such a hard time giving it to Him?

Two plain facts make trusting God difficult:
(1) Life is tough.
(2) We don't know the future.

If life were always easy, trusting God would be a cinch. Our life motto really could be "No problem, man." It's no problem to trust when there really are no problems.

Likewise, if we knew the future, trusting God would be simple. For example, when you are about to lose your job, if you could just look into the future and see that you actually will wind up with a better job in a different company, you could again say, "No problem. I don't need this job. God will take care of me." I don't get nearly as nervous watching the rerun of the final shot of my classmate Michael Jordan, securing the national championship for the Tarheels over Georgetown, as I did during the live game.

But life is tough, and we don't know the future. So we're left with trust.

The Bible has inspired the greatest art in the history of the world. Though I am certainly no expert, I am fascinated by artists' renderings of biblical scenes. Some paintings manage to capture the essence of a drama that is too high for words. Of course, no artist knows what these biblical characters actually looked like. But occasionally, a master captures the indescribable, delicate balance of contrasts between the creature and the Creator.

Such is Rembrandt's *Abraham and Isaac.*

My eyes were first drawn to his hands. Abraham's large, weathered left hand is blanketing his boy's face. All that is visible of Isaac's head are the youthful brown locks of hair dangling against the wood of the altar. The pressure of the patriarch's hand upon his son's face causes the boy's neck to be laid bare, stretched taut and upward—ready for a clean, quick incision.

Abraham's face, surrounded by white, receding hair and full beard, is furrowed with wrinkles of age, but still looks strong and determined. Quiet resolve.

But Abraham's determined face shows genuine surprise as well. The light floods the painting from the upper left corner. That is the direction from which it appears the angel flew. The heavenly messenger has broken through the dark, encompassing clouds which constitute the painting's background. The celestial light escapes through the clouds and shines brightly upon Abraham's face and upon the bare torso of his beloved son.

The angel must have appeared suddenly. The winged creature has grabbed the right wrist of the father by surprise. The gold-handled knife that was in Abraham's hand is falling impotently to the ground. The angel lifts the old man's hand upward as if to say, "This hand was not meant to slaughter but to bless."

Can you envision how Rembrandt caught the drama of that moment? Abraham's left hand is pressed to the altar. His right hand is caught by an angel. Therein is the human dilemma. As Christians, we're caught between Heaven's light and earth's darkness. Like Abraham, we are suspended between the inscrutable predicament of life and the amazing provision of God.

Oh, that the Christian life were only the holding of angels' hands. Oh, that it were only beams of heavenly light and never clouds of darkness.

But real life is both. God's provision is true, wonderful, and good. But the provision does not erase the predicament. Jesus said, "In this world you will have trouble" (John 16:33). You will not be immune to positive biopsies and persecuting business partners. Just as you may be blessed with unspeakable glory, you may be tested with agonizing trials.

If Abraham's left hand is attached to the predicament and his right is suspended by God's provision, what lingers between? Between the predicament and the provision is the bearer of the promise.

That's where we live most of our lives—clinging to the promise. Trusting that God will do what He has said He will do. Abraham did not know how God could make him the father of a nation if he sacrificed his only son. Abraham told Isaac, "God himself will provide the lamb" (Genesis 22:8). The author of the Book of Hebrews tells us that Abraham reasoned that God could bring Isaac back from the dead. Abraham did not know *how* God would provide, he just knew he *would* provide. Paul summarizes Abraham's trust: "He did not waver through unbelief regarding the promise of God, but was strengthened in his faith and gave glory to God, being fully persuaded that God had power to do what he had promised" (Romans 4:20–21).

That's what trust is—holding on to promises. That is, after all, how children live.

Isn't it amazing how your otherwise forgetful child can remember even your remotest promises? While you are getting four kids ready for the school bus, busily handing out lunches and knapsacks and bundling them up in their coats, your youngest asks, "Mom, can we go fly my new kite today?" Amidst the flurry of activity, you nod your head yes, but then you think no more of it. Your child, however, thinks of it all day.

She bursts into the house after school and cries out, "I'm home! Let's go fly my kite now!" Your excuses are interrupted by your child's greatest line of reasoning: "But you promised!"

Children live on promises. It's all they have to go on. They can't make things happen for themselves. They have to depend on bigger, stronger, richer adults to carry through on the promises they have made.

Between earth and Heaven, there's only one way a Christian can triumph: trusting God's promises. When life is its hardest, our most effective prayer sounds like this: "But, God, you promised!"

On one occasion, when Jesus was teaching His disciples about prayer, He pointed out a strange irony. "If you, then, though you are evil, know how to give good gifts to your children, how much more will your Father in heaven give good gifts to those who ask him!" (Matthew 7:11). We have it backward, Jesus is saying. Our children trust us more than we trust God. It ought to be the other way around. God has never broken a promise, but we earthly parents, sinners that we are, mess up all the time.

A woman in our congregation decided to trim her young son's hair. "No, Mommy," the little boy begged, "I'm afraid you'll cut my ear."

"Oh, don't be silly. Hush that talk. Of course I won't cut your ear," the mother insisted.

"Yes, you will. You will cut my ear."

"Be quiet," the now-agitated mom declared. "I promise I will not cut your ear."

With that promise still lingering in the air, she promptly took the scissors in hand, slipped them through her boy's hair, and snipped the flesh of his ear.

If children can so trust the promises of their sinful, ear-snipping parents, shouldn't you much more trust your Heavenly Father? He's the Giver of all good gifts. He's never once broken a promise. Never once made a mistake. Never once snipped an ear.

Whether or not you will trust God boils down to this: Do you really believe that your Heavenly Father has good in store for you? Children naturally trust that their parents really want what's best for them. My two-year-old may say "yuck" when I put green beans on his tray, but it would never cross his mind that I was trying to poison him.

Can you imagine the disastrous implications if an infant mistrusted his or her parents? Imagine if a baby could speak thoughts like these: "I'll not let you carry me across the street, Dad. You might throw me in front of a car." "I don't think I'll nurse today, Mom. Can't trust the milk...were you drinking last night?"

It is not necessary, nor even possible, to know how God will provide for your needs, but you must know that He will. And what He provides will be far better than what you could have provided for yourself.

My friend's brother worked as a waiter in a fine Atlanta restaurant. One evening a single man was seated at one of this waiter's tables. Seeing that the man was well-dressed and had the appearance of affluence, the waiter made sure to provide impeccable service. He went out of his way to double-check every detail of the man's meal. The customer's water glass was never below half-full. His bread plate never had less than two pats of butter. His food was delivered piping hot and presented with care. With hopes of a high tip, the waiter insured the customer an exquisite meal.

However, when the man concluded his dinner, the waiter was enraged by what he witnessed. The customer patted his mouth clean, pushed away from the table, and exited the restaurant. He just walked out. No payment for the meal. And worse—NO TIP!

Aghast, the furious waiter flew out after the seeming crook. The server leapt upon the customer, grabbed him by the collar, and began to shake a tip out of him.

"I gave you perfect service," the waiter shouted. "I served you an excellent meal. I can't believe that you have the audacity to walk out without so much as leaving me a tip. I demand that you give me what I deserve!"

The customer, seeking to save his own life, interrupted the waiter, "Hold on a minute, mister. Let go of my throat. Didn't your manager tell you? I *did* leave you a tip. And don't worry, I'm good for the bill. You see, I *own* this restaurant. I just came in tonight to see how things were going. You're right. The food *was* delicious. And your service *was* superb. If you'll find your manager when you go back in the restaurant, you'll discover I left you a hundred-dollar tip. Keep up the good work, son."

Gulp.

Have you ever treated God that way?

Maybe you've served the Lord faithfully. Maybe you've even given Him your all. But maybe you feel like you've been left staring at an empty table. Maybe you're wondering, "Where is He? Where has He gone? And where's the blessing I've always anticipated?"

Life is tough. Don't let anyone belittle your problems. It really does get hard sometimes.

You don't know the future, and neither do I. So it really does you no good to glibly say, "Everything will work out just like we want." It might not.

God really does provide. But right now you may be feeling a lot more of the predicament than the provision. Why would God let us feel the weight of that predicament? Why doesn't He just take away all our pain and fill us in on the details of our future?

Because God delights in our trust. He revels when we put the full weight of our lives in His arms. He rejoices when we see no tip on the table but go on to the next hungry soul, knowing the reward will eventually come. He likes it when we get to the end of our rope, get on our knees, and plead, "But, God...you promised."

CHAPTER SEVEN

Sleeping Like a Baby
Childlike Carefreeness

Do not be anxious about anything.

PHILIPPIANS 4:6

A wife bothered her husband every night of their seventeen years of married life saying, "Honey, wake up! I think I hear a burglar in the house."

Regularly, the dutiful husband stumbled downstairs, checked the empty house, returned to bed, and muttered, "No burglar."

One night, however, the husband happened upon an actual thief in the night. He politely asked the robber, "Before you finish packing up our family silver, would you mind coming upstairs with me? There's someone upstairs who has been waiting seventeen years to meet you."

The woman may have lost some household valuables that night, but she was the victim of a far worse crime. The real robber in that story was not a nighttime prowler but a much more dangerous predator. The real thief was worry.

Any common bandit can take your belongings, but worry can make you become *its* belonging.

In fact, worry is more than a thief—it is a mortal foe. Worry wages guerrilla warfare against the abundant life. It is wise to know your enemy.

- Worry's battleground—the mind
- Worry's battle cry—"What if...?"
- Worry's weapon—the lie
- Worry's tactic—one-on-one combat
- Worry's camouflage—concern
- Worry's nationality—hell

I know this enemy well. I have been on the front line against him. I've fallen to his sword before. I've seen how sharp is his blade and how deep his blow. I've watched my comrades fall and suffer. I've seen more than a few perish in the wake of worry's wrath.

This demonic warrior attacks the mind with deceptive suggestions. Like a broken record, he asks, "What if...?"

"What if you blow your big presentation? What if it costs you your job? What if you can't support your family?

"What if the doctor finds something strange during your physical? What if it's malignant? What if it's incurable? What if there's no treatment available?

"What if your child gets in with the wrong crowd? What if he gets on drugs? What if she gets pregnant? What if he drops out of school? What if she winds up in jail?

"What if...what if...what if...?"

This guerrilla-warfare foe drops no atomic bombs but prefers to locate the victim's weak spot and attack with tailor-made lies. As the etymology of the name suggests, worry likes to "choke" and "strangle."

Often painting himself as "necessary concern," worry doesn't want to kill you. He just wants to steal from you until he owns you.

Worry plays by no rules and is no respecter of persons. Rich. Poor. Successful. Struggling. Married. Single. Christian. Atheist. Elderly. Middle-aged. Young adult. Teenager. Worry attacks all, except...well, yes, there is one group that seems immune.

Little children.

Small children don't worry. Infants don't lie awake at night waiting for intruders. They sleep like...babies.

Sure, they feel pain like the rest of us. But they don't brood with gnawing anxiety. An infant has no concept of the word *dread*.

Our two-year-old doesn't even know he's going to the doctor until he gets there. Once he spies the white-smocked man with the stethoscope and the syringe, you'd better hold your ears. But it's over quickly, and Bennett doesn't even think about the doctor until the next check-up. It would never occur to him to worry about a disease that he doesn't have but could, theoretically, get.

To say children don't worry doesn't mean that they don't get scared. Toddlers can have nightmares. Even newborn babies demonstrate a protective reflex when they are startled. But worry is quite different from fright.

There may be an occasional benefit from fear. But worry is worthless. If a large, hungry lion jumps out of a cage at the zoo and starts running after you, a little fright might help speed up your old, tired legs. But worrying about the remote possibility that an unknown lion in a far-off zoo might escape and roam into your neighborhood provides you no help at all.

Mark Twain perhaps said it best: "I am an old man and have known a great many troubles, but most of them never happened."[1]

Worry's entire goal is to waste your life. So the culprit is quite satisfied to succeed with planting one good lie in you. One good, worrisome thought is enough to waste a whole night. Or a whole life.

A man complained to his next-door neighbor, "I haven't gotten any sleep because of your rooster crowing all night long."

"Why," the farmer replied, "that rooster doesn't crow all night. He crows only two or three times the whole night."

"I know," said the sleepless neighbor, "but I sit up in bed all night waiting for the next crowing."

But worry doesn't just keep you from going to sleep. It

keeps you from going...period. "An anxious heart weighs a man down," says Proverbs 12:25. It slows you down and ruins your effectiveness for Christ. It causes you to live a defensive life.

I bumped into an old acquaintance not long ago. "How are you doing?" I asked.

"Can't complain," he responded. "The wife and I are healthy. I didn't lose my job in the last round of layoffs at the company. Our daughter graduated from high school this year with no problems. A lot of girls in her school have gotten pregnant; we're so glad she hasn't. Our son's made it through middle school. You know how bad the drug use is among teenagers, but our boy has steered cleared of all that. So, all and all," he concluded, "things are going well."

Replay that conversation. I asked him how he'd been doing. He told me all the things that he had *avoided* doing. Is that the measure of a successful life? Let's see who can make it through life with the least number of worries coming true?

Worriers act as if life is nothing more than a minefield. Their only enjoyment is in avoiding the explosives. Their only goal is to make it through unharmed.

How different is the life of little children! For a toddler, life is not one big field of mines. It is one big field of dreams. Little children don't see life as an obstacle course. They see it as an opportunity.

Life is an opportunity to develop loving relationships. To learn new things. To impact souls. To change the world.

Can you imagine Jesus as a worrier?

"How are you doing, Jesus?"

"Well, things aren't going too well. I thought I had gotten off to a good start with my baptismal service and ordination ceremony. But I was severely attacked in the desert with all manner of temptation. I worry sometimes that I shouldn't be in the ministry. What if those temptations come back? What if I give in to temptation?

"I decided to go ahead with my calling, but I'm not sure if I have the gift of preaching. My first sermon was a bomb. Everybody at my hometown synagogue chased me out of town. If that's the way my friends treat me, I'm worried how my enemies will handle me.

"I do have some help, but I'm worried about these followers. They're not very educated. What if I invest all this time in them, and then they betray me?

"Also, I'm hearing a lot of rumblings from these Pharisees. They just don't like me. I'm worried because they influence a lot of people. Maybe I should just keep my distance from them, not ruffle anyone's feathers, and maybe they'll leave me alone. It's all pretty tough. Maybe I can make it through, though—if I don't hear any more talk of a cross...."

Maybe the reason Jesus accomplished so much in

three short years of ministry was that He never lost a minute to worry. He was the opposite of the old wit who said, "No wonder I'm so tired. I do everything three times. First, I worry about doing it. Then I do it. Then I rehash it in my mind, worrying whether I did it right."

The child with boundless energy lives the way Jesus did. It is the way He has commanded us to live: "Therefore do not worry about tomorrow, for tomorrow will worry about itself" (Matthew 6:34).

Have you ever noticed that the circumstance you long dreaded is never as bad as the worry itself? I see it regularly. Parishioners say, "I almost feel better now that I know it's malignant—the not knowing was so hard." What college student hasn't found the actual final exam to be less painful than the anxiety about failing it? The dread of a difficult conversation is far worse than the chat itself. The admission of guilt is a breeze compared to the agony of worrying whether someone will find out your sin.

Worry is almost always harder on us than even the worst real problems. Ever wonder why?

God gives grace only for actual needs, not for potential problems. The Lord's grace is "new every morning" (Lamentations 3:23). He grants grace to live each moment as you live it. When you are in the actual trial, God is with you. When you worry about tomorrow, you are on your own.

When Jesus was sending out his twelve disciples, He

warned them of some pretty unpleasant bumps in the road ahead: rejection, false accusation, public humiliation, flogging, trials before authorities. And then the Lord added, "But when they arrest you, do not worry about what to say or how to say it. At that time you will be given what to say" (Matthew 10:19).

"At that time." Not today. Not the day after. *"At that time."* The Greek words spell it out: "in that hour." It means "in that very instant."

How would you have responded to the Messiah's promise? "Uh, Lord, I really appreciate that good word. 'Preciate the encouragement and all, but, er...would you mind just sharing a little outline of what we're supposed to say *before* we're on trial? Just a little preview to ease my worry in the meantime? You don't have to give me the whole speech, but what about a few good sound bites I could memorize ahead of time?"

Most of us want tomorrow's grace today. But there is no answer for a problem that does not exist. God does not give solutions for hypothetical dilemmas. "Let us then approach the throne of grace with confidence, so that we may receive mercy and find grace to help us in our time of need" (Hebrews 4:16).

In your time of need, approach the throne of grace confidently. His love does not run out. His grace overflows. His mercy endures forever. In the moment that you need Him, which is every moment, He will meet you and meet your every need. But if you're looking for grace to help you through a crisis that has not yet arisen, and probably never will, good luck—you're on your own.

Are you tired of pouring your precious life down the drain of worry? Then it's time to become like a child. Do you remember that giant step backward in chapter 1? Here's another big dose of humility.

Little children don't worry about tomorrow because they know they have no control over tomorrow. My two-year-old keeps no DayTimer with tomorrow's appointment schedule. He does not watch the weather channel for the weekend forecast. He's never once wondered if the stock market would rally.

It's not that Bennett could care less what happens. Believe me, he'd much rather have an appointment with a birthday clown than a pediatrician. I'm sure he, too, prefers sunny days over drizzly ones. And I'm quite confident that he'd rather the stock certificate his granddaddy gave him would allow him to buy more toys, not fewer.

But still, little boys and girls give no thought to such matters—not because they don't care what happens tomorrow, but because they can't control what happens tomorrow.

If you are a worrier, you probably wish you had more control of the future. You probably think if you could do more, you'd worry less. You might think that if you had a little more confidence in yourself, you'd have a lot less anxiety about tomorrow.

It may sound odd, but finding a carefree life means losing confidence in yourself. I'm not talking about losing self-worth. You are worth more than you know. You are worth a King's descent and a Messiah's birth. You are worth a Savior's execution. You are worth everything to God. But you should have no more confidence in your ability to control your destiny than my toddler does his.

Sure, you can keep a DayTimer, and you ought to plan well. Sure, you can watch for dropping air pressure, and you ought not to pack a picnic with a hurricane on the way. Sure, you can watch the market, and you ought to guess when to buy and sell. But you are not in charge of tomorrow. And it's a good thing that you are not. I'm sure you are a wonderful person, but I wouldn't trust you with running the world for a minute. And you shouldn't trust yourself with it, either.

Have you looked upon the bliss of a sleeping baby and quietly longed for such tranquillity? Have you smiled at the unfettered silliness of a toddler and yearned for such freedom again? Then here's a wonderful offer: "Peace I leave with you; my peace I give you. I do not give to you as the world gives. Do not let your hearts be troubled and do not be afraid" (John 14:27).

It is not given as the world gives. It is not attained as

you might expect. He gives His peace not by granting you more confidence in yourself but by pointing out how frail you are. He gives His peace not by giving you more knowledge of the future but by reminding you of how little you know. He gives His peace not by taking away all your problems but by giving you all His grace.

Letting go of worry might require a miracle. But that's OK. God is good at miracles. Ask for His help. And if a worry-free life seems like something beyond comprehension, you're in good company. The apostle Paul couldn't explain it either:

> Do not be anxious about anything, but in everything, by prayer and petition, with thanksgiving, present your requests to God. And the peace of God, which transcends all understanding, will guard your hearts and your minds in Christ Jesus. (Philippians 4:6–7)

CHAPTER EIGHT

It's a Wonderful Life
Childlike Wonder

*Your works are wonderful,
I know that full well.*

PSALM 139:14

From the days of his youth, George Bailey knew what he was going to do. He was going to shake the dust off his feet, get out of his crummy, little hometown, and see the wonders of the world. He was going to lasso the moon for his girl, pack up that new suitcase his old boss gave him, and head out. One thing was for sure—George Bailey wasn't going to waste his life cooped up in a shabby loan office in Bedford Falls.

But poor George always found his adventure spoiled. Whether it was his father's stroke or his brother's marriage, something always kept Bailey in Bedford Falls. One by one, his wonderful dreams died. Finally, George decided he might as well die with his dreams.

The hero of Frank Capra's classic *It's a Wonderful Life*

stood on the bridge of despair. Overcome by the disappointment of crashed expectations, the depressed man prepared to hurl himself into the icy waters below.

Clarence, a novice angel, saved Bailey's body from drowning but, more importantly, saved his heart from despair. A magical journey back through time showed Bailey some marvelous moments in what he had considered a dreary life.

George Bailey recaptured love for life when he discovered a simple, profound truth: *The wonder of life does not depend on the location of the man but on the posture of the man's heart.*

The wonders of life need not be found in distant, exotic places. Wonder is as close as your own town, your own family, your own friends. Wonder can be rediscovered as quickly as the opening of your eyes.

I'm sure you're familiar with the trendy saying, "Been there. Done that."

I'm sure you know what it means too.

Been there...no reason to go back...seen one, seen 'em all...yawn.... Done that...no reason to do it again...doesn't do anything for me anymore...yawn...

Like all popular bumper stickers, the motto tells our tale. We live in a generation that thinks it's seen it all and done it all. Web browsers can get just about any piece of information they want whenever they want it. But you don't have to be a computer guru to participate in the communications explosion. And you don't have to be rich. It has affected almost everyone. A secondhand TV and a monthly cable payment gets you into somebody else's country, somebody else's economy, somebody else's war, somebody else's conversation, somebody else's sex life. So even if you haven't really seen much or done much, you feel like you have.

With so much knowledge, almost everyone finds little left to wonder about. Except for one small segment of society.

There is a group of people who know for sure that they *haven't* been there and *haven't* done much: little children. If an adult's motto is "Been there, done that," the toddler's motto is "I don't get to do anything!" A two-year-old's day is not guided by knowledge. It is led by wonder. When adults feel like they've seen it, done it, and know it all, children are left wondering about it all.

They're too small to see over the crowd, so they're left wondering what everybody is looking at. They haven't had enough education to understand it, so they wonder what those funny characters mean in books and on signs. And though they break a lot of things while dissecting them, children still wonder how things work and how they are made.

The secret to a wonderful life is as simple as the word itself: "wonder-full." A wonderful life is simply a life that is full of wonder. Adults find so little wonder. Children find it everywhere.

Many Christmases ago, when my brother did his routine peek into his daughter's bedroom to check on his sleeping three-year-old, he found her bed empty! A frantic search of the dark house concluded with this memorable sight. Little Courtney was sprawled out on her tummy in the living room. She had her favorite thumb in her mouth and her favorite blanket between her fingers. She, like the whole house, was still. In front of her glowed a newly decorated Christmas tree. Evidently, the tree's warm, colorful lights and glistening tinsel had wooed her from her bed and summoned her to wonder. She was not there to analyze the tree. She was there to wonder about it. She could not have identified the tree as Frazier fir or Scotch pine. She would not have been able to give you its price tag. She probably could not have told you why it was there. But there it was, glowing in the night. And her eyes were wide with wonder.

Just to appreciate the contrast, I'd like to have been a fly on the wall while her father erected the tree earlier that day. My eldest brother is a kind and patient man, but I've yet to see a man put up a Christmas tree with wonder in his eyes. For most men I know, a Christmas tree is more like a trophy awarded to a hunter than an object of beauty meant to elicit wondrous gazes. No, the tree is not valued for its wonder-evoking qualities. It is judged by its height, how long it keeps its needles, and most of all, its price. Some men have been known to drag their families to every tree lot in town to save $1.99.

The decorating of the tree is another battle to be won. It's something of an athletic feat—a contest to see who can erect the tree, string it with lights, and slap on those pesky ornaments the fastest. To the victor goes the spoils: more time in front of the NFL playoff game.

Surely (I'll give him the benefit of the doubt) my brother did not succumb to such Christmas tree antics. I do not know. I was not told. I was told only what his daughter did. She got lost in wonder.

It doesn't take Christmas to send a child into wonder.

Little children live in a state of wonder. Have you ever seen a baby girl who has just discovered her hands? Have you ever watched a toddler blow a bubble or inspect a strange bug? Have you ever stepped into an autumn night's air and heard your little boy say, "Look, Daddy, look! There's the moon up there!"? Have you noticed a child's glee to see a kite dance in the wind over a beach?

It's not the activity itself that brings such joy; it's the wonder that accompanies it. Adults haven't lost the ability to look at their hands, inspect bugs, spy the moon, or fly a kite. Grownups have lost the wonder that once accompanied such simple things.

Where, along the path to adulthood, did we lose our capacity to wonder?

The answer is as old as humanity. God made a man and gave him a garden. It was a beautiful, delectable garden: "The LORD God made all kinds of trees grow out of the ground—trees that were pleasing to the eye and good for food" (Genesis 2:9). And the Lord told the man that he was welcome to eat any fruit of any tree in the garden, except for one. One tree the man was not to taste. He was just to wonder about it. "You must not eat from the tree of the knowledge of good and evil, for when you eat of it you will surely die" (v. 17). But neither the man, nor his newly created mate was content to wonder. They wanted to *know*. And so they ate themselves sick.

God didn't make humans to be know-it-alls. He made us to be wonderers. Our chief sin has not changed: the pride of wanting to be our own gods.

Don't miss the tragedy of the drama. When Adam and Eve lost their wonder, they lost their lives.

Thankfully, the reverse is also true. If you can find wonder again, you can find life.

Jesse's youngest son tended sheep in the fields around Bethlehem. Neither his dad nor his family could, in their wildest dreams, ever have imagined that God would make him shepherd over all of Israel. In fact, when Samuel came to Jesse's house to anoint the new king, David wasn't even invited to the ceremony. But God chose him and called him "a man after my own heart" (Acts 13:22). God must have loved David's sense of wonder. A man who has much wonder has little pride. The less a man's pride, the more God can entrust to him. It was perhaps David's greatest virtue that he never ceased to marvel at God's love and power.

You can see it on almost every page of his psalms:

• "I...go about...telling of all your *wonderful* deeds" (Psalm 26:6–7).
• "Praise be to the LORD, for he showed his *wonderful* love to me" (Psalm 31:21).
• "Many, O LORD my God, are the *wonders* you have done" (Psalm 40:5).

Psalm 139 is David's pinnacle of wonder. Here he comes to his own mind's edge and finds his understanding falling helplessly below the unfathomable ways of God:

You hem me in—behind and before;
    you have laid your hand upon me.
Such knowledge is too wonderful for me,
    too lofty for me to attain.
For you created my inmost being;
    you knit me together in my mother's womb.
I praise you because I am fearfully and wonderfully
        made;
    your works are wonderful,
I know that full well.
                            (Psalm 139:5–6, 13–14)

Have you lost your wonder? Read Psalm 139. Keep reading it until you begin to feel what David felt. Consider a God who knows your thoughts before you think them. Consider how you've tried to escape Him and how He has not let you escape. Can you understand how God can be where you are going before you get there, or believe that He wants to be there even if it's a place you shouldn't be going?

Have you lost your wonder? Stretch out your hand. Consider the incredible intricacy of design that enables you to wiggle your fingers. Remember, for a moment, that you could wiggle those same fingers while in your mother's womb.

Have you lost wonder? I suggest you visit the newborn nursery at your local hospital. Stand at the nursery window and observe one-hour-old babies. Better yet, hold a sleeping baby and study his or her remarkable little life. Nothing makes me wonder more than the wonder of a "frame" that was "woven together" in God's "secret place."

At 3:19 A.M., September 27, I beheld the miracle of Matthew Bennett Wright's birth. Soon thereafter I had many more opportunities to behold him at 3:19 A.M. One early morning, the Lord cleared the sleep from my eyes and sent my soul into wonder with these words:

Bennett, I wonder
...if you'll ever know what a glorious nine years of marriage your parents spent before you were born, and if

you can see your father's love and respect for your mother grow with each passing day of parenthood?

...what was your favorite song that your parents sang to you while you were in the womb?

...if you know that before the brush of the first angel's wings in Heaven, your Creator had planned to make you and had set His love upon you?

...if the reason you look so deeply into my eyes when I whisper prayers over you is because an angel interprets for you?

...if God made your hands so big in order to be visible one day in the benediction over a congregation or to palm a basketball over an NBA net?

...if you noticed your father's teardrops fall on you when he held you first?

...if you know that your Creator also once wore diapers, cried with hunger at 4:00 A.M., and couldn't hold his head up by himself?

...if you sense that the only sadness in your father's heart is remorse over his own sin and that your birth has caused him to hunger for righteousness like you hunger for your mother's milk?

...if you can tell that your father loves you more than life itself, but that his Father loves you even more than that?

Bennett, mostly I wonder...how could God love me so much as to give me you?

Sleep well, little Bennett. While your father wonders...sleep well.

Dad

Wonder, like all childlike qualities, grows out of humility. Wonder comes only to the ones who see how big God is and how little we are. Wonder comes only to those who see how beautiful God is and how ugly we can be.

In recent years, the Lord has granted me overwhelming, holy, intimate moments in His presence. I've felt the weight of His glory like never before. I've been intoxicated with the joyous freedom of the Holy Spirit. I've heard His voice more clearly than I ever imagined possible. I've witnessed the power of His anointing.

I never realized that there was so much more of the life of Christ to experience. But with each new taste of His grace, I have only become hungry for more. With each new sip of His living water, I have only become more convinced that there is a whole river I've never seen. With each touch of His loving hand, I ponder more completely the fullness of Heaven's embrace.

The more you know God, the more you learn how much more of God there is to know.

The wonder-filled person is one who has heard God's question to Job: "Where were you when I laid the earth's foundation?" (Job 38:4) and been compelled to answer, "I don't know, Lord...haven't been there."

The wonder-filled person has heard God's question, "Have you ever given orders to the morning, or shown the dawn its place?" (v. 12) and been compelled to answer, "No, Lord...haven't done that."

The wonder-filled person has heard God's question, "Have you journeyed to the springs of the sea or walked in the recesses of the deep?" (v. 16) and been compelled to answer, "No, Lord...haven't been there."

The wonder-filled person has heard God ask, "Can you raise your voice to the clouds and cover yourself with a flood of water? Do you send the lightning bolts on their way?" (vv. 34–35) and responded, "No, Lord...haven't done that."

Do you see it now? It's odd, but don't miss it. It's not what you *have* seen and *have* done that makes your life marvelous. Instead, it's what you *haven't* seen and *haven't* done that makes life wonderful. Do you really want a wonderful life? It's time to let your adult "Been there, done that" change to a child's "I ain't seen nothin' yet!"

However, as it is written:

"No eye has seen,
    no ear has heard,
no mind has conceived
    what God has prepared for those who love him."
(1 Corinthians 2:9)

CHAPTER NINE

"Wow, Daddy!"
Childlike Astonishment

Remember the wonders he has done.

1 CHRONICLES 16:12

I love to see my little boy look astonished. Here are some things that amaze him:

• I can easily slam-dunk his miniature basketball on his plastic Little Tikes basketball goal even at its highest setting. When I perform this awesome feat, my boy shouts, "Hooray, Daddy!" and dances a jig in celebration. (One day he'll discover that at five-foot-eight, his daddy can barely touch the net on a real goal and that ESPN has no Little Tikes slam-dunk contest.)

• I can crush a Cheerio by the sheer act of brute force using only my thumb and forefinger. I usually grunt and groan a little for added effect while squeezing the helpless Cheerio. When I perform this Samson-like stunt, my boy claps his hands and squeals with delight. (One day he'll discover that I'm not Mr. Universe and that sometimes I can't get the pickle jar open without banging on the lid with a spoon.)

• I can build a tower of blocks that is taller than he is. When I construct these skyscrapers, Bennett shouts, "Wowee!" and jumps about until the flimsy structure topples over. (One day my little boy will discover that these stacks of blocks are the first thing I've built since the backgammon board I made in high school shop.)

I'll do about anything to elicit that joyous look of childlike surprise on his face. Sometime ago, I put a piece of candy in a small box and shook it vigorously in front of Bennett.

"A surprise for Bennett! A surprise for Bennett!" I shouted with enthusiasm. I led him on a chase around the playroom just long enough to make it fun, then I let him open the little box. I wouldn't take a million dollars for the look on his face when he saw that morsel of his favorite candy inside.

Ever since, when I shake the little box, Bennett comes running. Most of the time when he opens it, he finds only a toy screwdriver, a miscellaneous puzzle piece, or an old golf ball. But he's never disappointed because he knows that next time there might be a piece of chocolate inside.

I'm convinced that God the Father delights in astonishing His children.

Why did God divide the Red Sea for His children?

Sure, He wanted to save them from the pursuing Egyptians. But couldn't He have accomplished the same purpose with a little simpler, less showy act? He could have set a pesky brush fire in the Egyptians' path or sent in some neighboring nation's army to help Israel fight. But no. God rolled back the sea's mighty waters right in front of His children. Maybe He just wanted to see the look on their faces.

And why did He order Joshua to march around Jericho in such strange fashion? Wouldn't an ordinary battering ram have done the trick? Maybe the Lord just wanted to hear His children's shouts of amazement when the walls fell to the sound of trumpets.

And wasn't Jesus surprising? His first miracle saved no sinners, healed no sick, delivered no oppressed. He just made about 180 gallons of wine for a party. Why did He do it? John summed it up: "He thus revealed His glory" (John 2:11).

And what about this walking on water? What's wrong with boats? And, besides, it was after 3:00 A.M. Why not wait until daybreak? Of course the disciples were astonished. In fact, the Bible says they thought they had seen a ghost. The Lord quickly calmed them, reassuring them that it was only He. But what did Jesus expect? If you go walking on the water through heavy waves in the middle of the night, you can expect a little amazement in the eyes of your beholders.

The Heavenly Father wants His children to live in astonishment. Though He has offered us deep intimacy with Him and has welcomed us into the throne room itself, we must never lose our astonishment at His eternal majesty. We cannot know God except through the child-like eyes of astonishment.

Because God loves for us to be astonished at His goodness and glory, human beings will never be satisfied until they are astonished. If we were honest, most of us would admit that life can get boring pretty quickly. We would confess that we desperately long for something new, something surprising, something amazing to invade our otherwise mundane lives.

Many years ago, a religious scholar discovered a remarkable truth about human encounters with the holy. When encountering the holy, there is first a sense of great awe, even terror. He called it *mysterium tremendum*—the tremendous mystery. But there is, at the same time, a strange attraction. He called it *mysterium fascinans*—a mysterious fascination.[1]

This fascination is probably the key to why people like horror movies. Girls clutch their dates and hide their eyes at the scariest parts of the movie. But they also peek, just enough to see what happens. The very thing that is most frightening is, oddly, most attractive. That's why kids love dinosaurs. Who wouldn't tremble to hear the pounding of a Tyrannosaurus Rex's clawed feet upon the ground? But who wouldn't want at least a glimpse of the carnivore?

Let's face it. We crave astonishment. How else can you explain the popularity of the sideshows at the state fair? Walking through the North Carolina state fairgrounds you can hear megaphones barking out some astonishing claims:

• *The Decapitated Starlet!* Come one, come all! A beautiful girl driving along a California highway was in a horrible accident. She was thrown through the windshield and decapitated. Doctors immediately rushed her to UCLA Medical Center, where they worked around the clock to keep her body alive. Today, here, now, you can see the product of their work. Miss Tracy Steel is still alive, but without a head! You will see her move her legs, her arms, her hands and feet. Her body is still alive!

• *Venom!* Randy Richards was turned on to drugs, turned into an animal, and turned off for life. He's half-animal, half-human. Randy Richards, banned from society forever, condemned to a living death—and still alive. He's alive, alive, alive! He's locked in a steel cage. During an earthquake, his home was destroyed. He lived under the city of Los Angeles for twenty years. He was found wandering the streets with a nine-foot boa constrictor wrapped around his body. Attempts to put clothes on his body are almost impossible.[2]

I won't tell you about Angel the Snake Girl or Zahara the Gorilla Girl. I'm sure you get the picture.

If you can't get to the state fair, you need go no further than your local supermarket to be astonished. The tabloids alert you to all the space aliens, fifty-pound newborns, and twenty-foot giants around. And have you noticed that some of the most popular TV shows are ones that feature astonishing stories? Harrowing rescues, unsolved crimes, and bizarre mysteries rank high. People don't want just regular news anymore, they want astonishing news.

Our young people are still starved for astonishment. The most recent studies show dramatic increases in teen drug use. They're still looking for something new, something surprising, to break the sheer boredom of life.

Part of our problem is that we're so forgetful. What amazed us yesterday may bore us today. You might cruise right by things that once stopped you in your tracks. Things that once made your eyes pop out, now may just help you get some shuteye.

How can the groom who once nearly fainted just to see the beauty of his bride moving down the aisle later not care to lift his eyes from the newspaper at the kitchen table? How can the father who wept upon seeing his first-born arrive in the world later scream at the child, "I wish you'd never been born!"? How can a child who grew up saying, "Wowee, Daddy! Do that again!" shrug his teenage shoulders and say, "Big deal, Dad. I gotta go now"?

Though the Israelites were astonished when the plagues beset Pharaoh and when the Red Sea parted, God knew His children had short memories. The Lord knew that His people would need help remembering how He set them free, so He said of the Passover, "This is a day you are to commemorate; for the generations to come you shall celebrate it as a festival to the LORD—a lasting ordinance. Celebrate the Feast of Unleavened Bread, because it was on this very day that I brought your divisions out of Egypt" (Exodus 12:14, 17).

In fact, the Scriptures are filled with God's warnings not to forget:

• "Remember the wonders he has done, his miracles, and the judgments he pronounced. Declare his glory among the nations, his marvelous deeds among all peoples" (1 Chronicles 16:12, 24).

• "Only be careful, and watch yourselves closely so that you do not forget the things your eyes have seen or let them slip from your heart as long as you live. Teach them to your children and to their children after them" (Deuteronomy 4:9).

• "Remember that you were slaves in Egypt and that the LORD your God brought you out of there with a mighty hand and an outstretched arm" (Deuteronomy 5:15).

Nehemiah summed up the failing of God's people: "They refused to listen and failed to remember the miracles you performed among them" (Nehemiah 9:17).

Jesus didn't want you or me to forget, either: "And he took bread, gave thanks and broke it, and gave it to them, saying, 'This is my body given for you; do this in remembrance of me'" (Luke 22:19).

Children are not only more easily astonished, but they also stay astonished a lot longer. Amazingly, if I crush a Cheerio between my thumb and forefinger five times, in Bennett's eyes the fifth time is just as marvelous as the first. And children remember the look of fury in their parents' eyes. I'm sure our boy remembers the look on my face after he pelted me with his juice cup in the back of the head as I was driving on Interstate 85. I'm sure he remembers how fast a father can pull on to the nearest exit ramp and how quickly that father can get a little boy out of his car seat. The spanking was gentle, but the father's face was, I'm sure, astonishing. Bennett's not hurled his juice cup at me again.

The Christians who live the most abundant lives are those with the best memories. They remember what it was like to be lost in sin. They remember what God has done for them. They remember the miracles He has performed. They live in astonishment that God could love them so much. They remain surprised that God would have mercy on them.

Roger loves God, and he loves me. I like being around him because his spiritual appetite whets mine as well.

Roger is more than a parishioner; he is a prayer partner. When we pray, he often gets on his knees and weeps for love of the Lord and the desire for His church to be blessed. He loves and respects God's Word. He is a respected teacher and an exemplary church leader. He loves his wife deeply and nurtures his children in the precious ways of God. His humble manner endears him to almost everyone.

In short, Roger is every pastor's dream parishioner.

But Roger always felt like he was missing something. He knew that God worked miracles, but it seemed that those supernatural moments were always happening somewhere else for someone else, through someone else. Because he had experienced no dramatic, Pentecostal infilling, he wondered if something was wanting in his spiritual life.

Some of us tried to convince Roger that God was powerfully at work in his life and that the Lord was truly using him to bless others in dramatic ways. On more than one occasion, I tried to convince Roger that I'd love a congregation full of people just like him. And it was true. I'd take a whole congregation of Rogers who honestly love God and love the body of Christ over a church full of puffed-up parishioners who think they are the spiritually elite. But still, Roger had doubts about his spiritual life.

Until one day the Lord spoke to him.

It wasn't the kind of dramatic experience that Roger had heard others talk about. It was a quiet experience. And it wasn't ecstatic. There was no rapturous vision. No audible voice. No angelic visitation.

Instead, Roger simply met with a few prayer counselors after a conference worship service. He shared how he hungered for God and wanted God's leading more than anything. In the midst of their prayer time, one of the counselors quietly confided, "Roger, I believe the Lord has given me a word for you. I'm not sure what all it means. But I believe it is something the Lord really wants you to know and to believe."

He then shared some words that would change this man's life: "Roger, you are going to be astonished."

Believing the message to be authentic, Roger was excited, and so was I. We figured God was about to do some astounding new thing in his life. But no unbelievable miracle or ecstatic experience was forthcoming.

Only later did I realize that God was giving Roger something altogether different from what we had supposed. And this gift was altogether better.

Over time it became clear. God was already doing marvelous things in and through Roger. What he needed most was the ability to realize it. He needed his eyes opened to the astonishing acts of God taking place all around him.

God did not change. Roger did. God didn't suddenly start working miracles. Roger just began noticing them more. It began in small ways. "I think that was the Lord at work," he would say. Or, "Let me tell you about this answered prayer." Soon Roger began sharing marvelous testimonies of God's power at work.

Every now and then I smile at him and say, "Why, Roger, that sounds downright—astonishing!"

We have a mighty big God who does mighty big things. He speaks the word and whole worlds are formed. He points a finger and legions of angels are dispatched. He waves His hand and oceans dance. He opens His arms and sinners lose their sin. Our God is King of Kings and Lord of Lords. He is Ruler of all and ruled by none. His glory is ineffable, His beauty unimaginable. The Lord God is astonishing.

The only question is, are you astonished? Or do you shrug your shoulders?

If you've never found grace amazing, you've not found grace.

If you've never found forgiveness bewildering, you've not seen the cross.

If you've never found the answer, you've not asked

with Charles Wesley's hymn: "Amazing love how can it be, that You, My God, wouldst die for me?"

To become like a child again, look at your sin and remember what you were; look at the cross and remember what He did; look up to Heaven and say, "Wow!"

CHAPTER TEN

"Naked As the Day You Were Born"

Childlike Transparency

*And they hid from the LORD God
among the trees of the garden.*

GENESIS 3:8

The other day my wife and I were at the mall pushing our two-year-old in the stroller when he made the unpleasant announcement, "I have a stinky diaper." We weren't near any bathroom and were in a bit of a hurry. Though we aren't usually prone to such tackiness, we got lazy and decided just to change the boy on a bench in the middle of the mall. Though we completed the task in record time, I felt uncomfortable. I didn't even look at the shoppers who happened by, but unless they had some severe nasal congestion, I'm sure they were a bit uncomfortable as well.

As we continued strolling, I chuckled and asked my wife, "Can you even imagine someone laying you down amidst a heavy-traffic area in the mall, pulling off your clothes, grabbing your ankles, and lifting your freshly soiled bottom up high for cleaning?"

No comment.

The only one who was perfectly happy was Bennett himself. Not only did he make no protest, but I was a little concerned that he might begin to shout, "Look, everybody, I have a stinky diaper!" I'm sure he would have been exceedingly happy if we had allowed him to spring down from the bench diaperless so he could bound about the mall as naked as the day he was born.

I'm no nudity advocate. Jesus wore clothes (remember the hemorrhaging woman touched the hem of his garment), and that's more than enough reason for me to wear clothes too. But isn't there something utterly delightful about the complete lack of shame in a little child? Little children not only see no need for clothes to cover their bodies but are equally unconcerned about camouflaging their emotions. It's never hard to tell what a toddler is thinking or feeling. And though it catches us off guard sometimes, their unfogged transparency is oh, so refreshing.

On the pathway to adulthood, we learn to cover ourselves up. Some modesty is essential, of course. And it is foolish to blab our deepest secrets to the common sinner on the street. But we learn to play the hiding game too well. Everyone I know hides well. Only a few know how to be found.

As a little girl, my niece once hid from the baby-sitter. It started as a cute little game, I'm sure. She was hiding in a very good spot, and the baby-sitter couldn't find her. But as time went on, the game got to the point where it wasn't funny anymore. The baby-sitter couldn't find little Courtney anywhere. Finally, the panicked sitter frantically called the neighbor. The caring neighbor promptly came over and slowly, loudly declared to the silent house, "Courtney, this is Lisa's mom. I know you are hiding somewhere in the house, and I think you had better come out right away." It didn't take long for the little girl to emerge.

I'm sure she was more scared than the baby-sitter. What had started out innocently had turned frightening. The longer she hid, the harder it was to quit hiding. The longer the silence, the greater the shame. The longer she was there, the more her hiding place felt safe. But had she continued to hide, she would have never received the things she needed and wanted most in life, like food, hugs, friends, love, and learning.

Hiding would eventually have destroyed her. Hiding will always eventually ruin us.

Consider the couple who sat in my study not long ago. They have three darling children. Two good jobs. A lovely home. Many good friends. A caring church. But almost no marriage. He drops a bomb.

"I don't know if I want to be married to her anymore."

The weight of the words descend upon the woman's small shoulders. "I don't understand," she says. "I thought we were a happy family."

"You've been married thirteen years; how long have

you been feeling this way?" I ask the man.

"Years. I think I got married for all the wrong reasons." He drops another bomb: "Maybe I've never really loved her."

"Why haven't you told her this before?" I probe.

"I guess I just didn't want to hurt her."

She is quiet. I speak softly. "I'm sure she couldn't be hurt more than she is now."

Skilled mask wearers can hide their hearts for years. Without a miracle, the marriage is doomed. Had there been transparency years earlier, they might have been helped. But there was never any real communication. Without sharing, there is no relationship. Without transparency, there is no intimacy.

The healthiest people are also the most transparent people. They aren't necessarily the most pleasant people to be around, but recent studies show that people who repress their emotions have a significantly higher risk of heart disease.[1] Worse than the physical heart disease, though, is the degeneration of the spiritual heart.

That's what Jesus was most concerned about.

The Savior did not hide His emotions. When He was sad, He wept. In fact, when describing Jesus at Lazarus's tomb, John uses a Greek word that means He shook with deepest emotion. When Christ was angry, he turned over moneychangers' tables and started cracking a whip. When the seventy-two returned to tell Jesus how excited they were about the power of God working through them, Luke says Jesus was "full of joy" (Luke 10:21). His face must have shown it. I imagine He laughed or shouted out loud.

The Messiah wore no mask and had no patience with those who did.

Jesus had the perfect word to describe such hiding: *hypocrisy.* The ancient Greeks loved drama. They would crowd into large amphitheaters for comedies and tragedies. The scripts were sometimes masterpieces, but the productions wouldn't have won any awards for special effects. The actors had only one visual aid: They each held a mask in front of their faces. The Greek word for such mask-wearing actors was *hypokrites.*

That seems to be Jesus' favorite word for the Pharisees. The Lord calls the Pharisees hypocrites six times in Matthew 23 alone. The word fit the mask-wearing religious leaders perfectly. During feast time, the local authorities would paint the tombs so pilgrims would see clean, white cemeteries as they walked into town. On the outside, the Pharisees looked spotlessly clean. On the inside, Jesus said they were full of decay.

The Lord is not content to leave you in hiding. He never has been.

Before they disobeyed God, Adam and Eve didn't even know they were naked. Though it's hard to imagine, they would have been quite content to have their bottoms lifted up on a public bench or in a busy mall. They didn't even know what shame was until they ate the deadly fruit. The Bible describes the Fall quite succinctly: "Then the eyes of both of them were opened, and they realized they were naked; so they sewed fig leaves together and made coverings for themselves" (Genesis 3:7).

They hid from one another. And they hid from God: "Then the man and his wife heard the sound of the LORD God as he was walking in the garden in the cool of the day, and they hid from the LORD God" (v. 8).

But God had made these creatures for a purpose. He had created them for fellowship with their Creator. He wanted their worship. He wanted their fellowship. He wanted their love. He wanted them to share their most intimate thoughts and desires. He would not be satisfied until this man and woman, made in His image, came out of hiding. So the Lord asked what one preacher has called the "primal question."[2] It was the first question that God had ever asked. It is the most important question God has ever asked. It is the question that every human being must eventually answer. It is the question that God asks you even now:

"Where are you?"

When He asks, "Where are you?" it is for your sake, not His. The Lord knows exactly where you are. But He wants you to be free. God is no more content to leave you in hiding than He was with Adam and Eve. Though it may not be comfortable, He will send His Spirit to search you out. If He has to, He will lay you bare.

Unbeknown to me, my wife invited a troubled friend to church. She was an old school friend; Anne learned that she had suffered a bad marriage and was experiencing numerous other personal struggles. After months of Anne's inviting her, the woman finally attended church one Sunday morning. I didn't know that she was there and knew nothing of her plight.

After the service, however, the woman was indignant. In her deep agitation, she cornered my wife and berated her: "You told him everything, didn't you?"

"What are you talking about?" Anne questioned.

"You know exactly what I am talking about. I confided my problems to you, and you told every bit of it to your husband. He obviously knew I was coming today. He couldn't have preached that sermon if you hadn't told him."

She never came back to church. She never believed that Anne hadn't told me all about her.

I didn't know her situation. But the Holy Spirit did. I wasn't exposing her. God was. Actually, that sort of thing happens a lot. Except usually, when the Holy Spirit lays bare a soul, the soul comes back to church.

As much as we want to hide, we want even more to be found.

Hiding makes us feel safe. Life seems bearable that way. But it is altogether unfulfilling. And it is painfully lonely.

Our toddler loves to play a little hiding game with us. In plain view, he giggles and runs to the living room to hide. There is, of course, no mystery involved. He always hides in the exact same spot—between the couch and end table. But, regularly, Anne and I call out, "B-e-n-n-e-t-t!" We hear little chuckles from behind the couch. Then we question one another, "Anne, have you seen Bennett any-where?"

"No, I haven't seen him. Where could he be?"

Together we question the air in loud voices, "Has *any-one* seen Bennett?"

In asking the question the other day, a little voice emerged from under the end table. "Nobody."

The point of the hiding game is not the hiding—it is the finding. It is pure joy to be found and still be loved. The gospel's good news is that you can come out of hiding and still be loved. Look who Jesus loved: a woman openly caught in adultery, a publicly hated tax collector, a known prostitute, an unclean woman who touched his garment in a crowd, some uneducated fishermen, blind beggars, a condemned thief on a cross, outcast lepers, little children. Ironically, the only ones Jesus deemed to be in eternal dan-ger were the ones still in hiding.

You might be good at hiding. But Jesus is better at

finding. He came "to seek and to save what was lost" (Luke 19:10). Why not take the mask off—and be found?

CHAPTER ELEVEN

The Naked Truth

Childlike Candor

*Speaking the truth in love, we will in all things grow up
into him who is the Head, that is, Christ.*

EPHESIANS 4:15

What parent hasn't turned crimson in the wake of his or
her toddler's unguarded honesty?

Maybe it's happened to you in the grocery store check-
out line. It starts with the toddler's gawking stare at the
cashier's unkempt hair. Then, in a voice loud enough for
the butcher in the back of the store to hear, your little girl
points and shouts, "What's wrong with her hair?" If that's
not bad enough, most toddlers persist with their keen
observations: "Look, Mommy, look. That lady's hair is
funny! See her hair, Mommy?" There is no gracious way
out of such scenes. The best strategy is to pretend you are
just baby-sitting the child. Or, better yet, pretend that
you've never seen the child before: "Where is this girl's
mother?"

No subject matter is off-limits to a child's candor.

Children will openly describe their body parts and functions. In front of both teacher and parent, one of my wife's kindergartners once described his crayon drawing as "Mommy and Daddy in the shower." If I've been sweating, my niece never hesitates to tell me that I stink. When he would prefer to be with Mommy, my own toddler regularly tells me, "Go away, Daddy. Go away."

Adults have learned that, though such candor may be cute at times, it is no way to win friends and influence people.

I remember the family gathering to watch five-year-old Christopher tear into his birthday presents. My wife and I were excited about our gift to our fun-loving nephew—a miniature foozball game. But when he had opened the box wide enough to see its contents, Christopher's face contorted as if he were swallowing cough syrup. With disgust, he openly declared, "Ooh! I hate these things!"

The family members managed embarrassed smiles and collectively muttered something about this just being a phase. Christopher's parents gasped and explained that no one would want to give him any more presents if he reacted like that. Their ensuing lessons on gratitude were well in order, but Christopher began learning another lesson that we've all been taught: *If you want to get anywhere in this world, don't tell anyone what you really think.* And so most of us grow up believing the worst thing we can do is expose our true feelings.

I think my southern upbringing exacerbated the problem for me. In the South, where hospitality and politeness rank especially high, people don't blurt out their thoughts. If you drop by a neighbor's house on a hot, July afternoon, it takes some considerable time just to get a glass of iced tea.

"Hello, friend. How 'bout a glass of iced tea?" your neighbor asks.

You're parched, but you respond properly, "Oh no, I'm fine. Wouldn't want to put you to any trouble."

"It's no trouble," the hospitable neighbor declares. "I'd love to pour you a glass."

"No, no, I don't want to be a bother," you are obliged to respond.

"Really, it's no trouble," the neighbor then insists. "I've got the glass out; the tea is already brewed. I'm going to have a glass. Please join me."

"Well," your dry lips are now allowed to concede, "if you're having some…maybe I'll have half a glass."

If my parents' teaching and my southern culture were not enough to make me nice and polite, then my Christian mentors were sure to seal it. The evangelical ministry that fostered my early relationship with Christ rightly emphasized the importance of personal witness. We talked about others seeing Christ in us and would often say, "Be careful how you live; others are watching, and you may be the only Bible those people will ever read."

I figured it worked this way: If I could just be nice enough on a regular basis, then people would marvel at my kindness, figure I must have Christ in me, and therefore would want to become nice Christians too.

In seminary, I learned a model of pastoral care and counseling that reinforced my nice nature. It was called reflective listening and nondirective counseling. It works this way:

Someone says, "Pastor, I feel like killing my mother-in-law. What should I do?"

The counselor should respond, "Hmm, tell me more. It sounds as though you are angry at your mother-in-law."

When the counselee affirms, "Yep, I really do want to kill her," the counselor should follow with, "How do you feel when you think of killing her?"

"The thought feels really great, Pastor. Do you think I should go ahead and kill her?"

"Hmm…what do you think?"

I exaggerate, of course. But it didn't take long in the ministry to realize that people want a "nice" pastor more than they want an honest pastor. Most of the pastors I know are really nice people. So are most of the parishioners. I know a lot of really nice Christians. But I know only a handful of really honest ones. I know almost none who have the unguarded candor of a little child. Something happens along the pathway to adulthood that makes most of us phony.

How different is our Lord Jesus.

In His lengthy speech of Matthew 23, He openly calls the Pharisees blind guides, whitewashed tombs, snakes, and vipers. With raw candor, Jesus blurts out His deep disgust with their whole way of life and scorns the religious system they had spent their lives perfecting: "Woe to you, teachers of the law and Pharisees, you hypocrites! You give a tenth of your spices—mint, dill and cummin. But you have neglected the more important matters of the law—justice, mercy and faithfulness" (v. 23).

This is not the way I was taught to preach. Good preachers emphasize the positive. If you must point out sin and error, couch it carefully amid a lot of talk about grace and forgiveness. And if you must confront people personally with their faults, be sure to point out all their strengths first.

Jesus would have scored a higher grade in most of our seminaries if He had conducted Himself more like this: "Excuse me, Pharisees, would you mind if I scheduled an appointment to meet with you? There is a private matter I would very much like to discuss. I know you are very busy, and I don't want to intrude upon your time. Also, the matter which I want to address does not need to be overheard by anyone else.... Two o'clock tomorrow...in your study...very good. I'll see you then.

"Thank you, Pharisees and teachers of the law, for seeing me. You are so kind to grant me this audience. What I have to say today will hurt me more than it hurts you. I have such respect for you in so many ways. The way that you know God's Word from cover to cover and your zealous spirit for keeping the law make me appreciate your noble attempt to be the very best religious leaders that you can be. Please remember, the things I am about to say do not diminish my genuine respect and appreciation for your work. There is one little matter about your religious leadership. How shall I put it? Might there be a little part of your appearance that might not be totally genuine? I-I-I don't want to offend...I just want to start a little dialogue about the subject."

The Lord never speaks this way. Jesus' words are relentless, and He doesn't soften them by adding any positive points about the Pharisees. He comes brashly to the point: "Woe to you, teachers of the law and Pharisees, you hypocrites! You are like whitewashed tombs, which look beautiful on the outside but on the inside are full of dead men's bones and everything unclean" (v. 27).

Jesus caps off His sermon with this uplifting thought: "How will you escape being condemned to hell?" (v. 33).

If someone showed up in one of our nice evangelical churches talking this way, we would dub such behavior "unChristlike." We'd probably inform him he was blowing his witness and disrupting the peace of the church. Be honest. If you are a clean-cut, meek, nonconfrontational, "nice" Christian, you'd never say such things to anyone, no matter how much you felt like speaking your mind.

What made Jesus so different?

The Messiah had no need for human approval. The Heavenly Father didn't teach His Son what to say in order to get along well in the world. Jesus never adjusted His language to get more approval for His mission. He never once hobnobbed with the elite or buttered up the politicians with hopes that they might help His cause. Jesus refused to compromise truth for the sake of personal comfort.

Since you're reading this nice Christian book, chances are you are a nice person. You probably say a lot of nice things to people and do a lot of nice things for them as well. Wonderful. But let me ask you with as much candor as I can muster: Why are you so nice?

Is it because you are overflowing with genuine love and affection for people? Or is it because you're afraid that if you offend them, they may not like you anymore?

Employees, why do you tell your boss that you like his leadership style? Do you want to encourage him with honest feedback or get a promotion?

Husbands, why do you tell your wife she looks beautiful? Is it because your heart still skips a beat when she passes by? Or do you just want some physical gratification?

Wives, why do you fold your husband's clothes? Because you delight in humble service or because you fear more of his criticism?

Store clerks, why do you tell your customer that the

blouse looks just great on her? Do you really see beauty, or do you want a quick sale?

Let's face it. Most of us are phony, and we live in a world filled with phonies. Strange as it may sound, a lot of evangelical Christians are too nice. You might be too nice if…

• You leave a good tip even when the service was lousy.

• You laugh at a joke that wasn't even funny.

• You smile and vote yes during the committee meeting and then congregate in the parking lot to grumble about the board's decision.

• You quit your job because of the business's unethical practices, but you told no one why you quit.

• Your husband is an alcoholic, but you've never told anyone in order to protect his reputation.

• When someone asks you how you're doing, you automatically say "fine," even if you're on your way to the pharmacy to pick up your Prozac refill.

I'd like to say that Jesus' candor was deemed cute, like a child's. But the rebuked leaders did not think Jesus cute at all. When a toddler blurts out the raw truth, some people blush. When an adult speaks the truth, some people get mad. Hypocrites don't want their masks taken away. Phonies don't want to be exposed. The religious and political rulers of Jesus' day decided to crucify the candor rather than remove their masks.

This great urge to silence the truth was not new:

"I am sending you prophets and wise men and teachers. Some of them you will kill and crucify; others you will flog in your synagogues and pursue from town to town. O Jerusalem, Jerusalem, you who kill the prophets and stone those sent to you, how often I have longed to gather your children together, as a hen gathers her chicks under her wings, but you were not willing." (Matthew 23:34, 37)

Though Jesus' candor cost Him worldly comfort, it brought salvation to all who had ears to hear the truth. It is only by knowing the truth that we are set free. If you wanted to visit me in my North Carolina home, wouldn't you want specific directions to my house? In fact, the more narrow and specific the directions, the better. Which is better, to say, "Oh, just come to western Winston-Salem," or to send you a map with every street name highlighted? The reason Jesus was so committed to truth was because He wanted no one to be lost.

Let's be honest. The reason we lack candor is not because we want to protect others. We want to protect ourselves. Real love always speaks the truth.

But real truth must always be spoken in love.

I preached on the subject of honesty to my congregation

one Sunday morning. Several people told me on the way out that they didn't like my tie. A few told me the sermon stunk. They were joking, I think. But I did begin to regret ever preaching the sermon. After all, I have such a friendly congregation. Each Sunday morning I ask worshipers to turn to their neighbors and give them a warm greeting. I don't tell them to turn to their neighbors and speak their mind. I really don't want them saying to one another, "Ugly tie, viper" and "Not as ugly as your face, white-washed tomb."

Candor must never be cruel. Even Jesus' incisive honesty with the Pharisees was a surgeon's scalpel that held the possibility of great healing.

A doctor does no favor to a patient by ignoring a cancer and issuing a false report of health. Christians do one another no favors by pretending that all is well. The body of Christ cannot mature without candor. The apostle Paul taught the Ephesians this principle: "Speaking the truth in love, we will in all things grow up into him who is the Head, that is, Christ" (Ephesians 4:15).

Truth. Love. Where one goes, the other must go. Truth without love is sadism. Love without truth is irrelevant. Christ perfectly embodied both.

With a talkative boy who has just turned two, I'm sure Anne and I have plenty more embarrassing moments ahead of us. I don't relish opportunities for my boy to point out clownish hairdos, obtrusive noses, and large derrières. But I don't want him to lose his candor. I think I'd prefer a few embarrassing moments instead of a life-time of phoniness. Doesn't this world need more Christians who will call sin "sin"? Don't we long for a few more leaders who are more committed to truth than they are to opinion polls?

Isn't it time to start speaking your mind without worrying about what others will think? Say what you mean, and mean what you say. Exchange your phoniness for candor. You'll have to if you want to become like a child. You'll have to if you want to be like Jesus.

Grace, mercy and peace from God the Father and from Jesus Christ, the Father's Son, will be with us in truth and love. (2 John 3)

CHAPTER TWELVE

Make-Believers and Belief Makers

Childlike Imagination

"I tell you the truth, anyone who has faith in me will do what I have been doing. He will do even greater things than these."

JOHN 14:12

What do you get when you mix the mind of a genius with the heart of a child? You get someone bound to change the world. Someone like Lee Bryan.

One Sunday after church he asked me, "What's the difference between humans and animals?"

He asked it casually, like a child rehearsing a knock-knock joke. But I knew he had an idea, and I wanted to hear it. Lee always gets a good return on his ideas. He's the only guy I know who has million-dollar ideas, literally.

"What's the difference?" I asked hungrily.

"Imagination," Lee said with a smile. "That's the difference. Humans can envision things that don't exist. Animals can't."

Lee Bryan speaks with authority on the subject because he is, among other things, an inventor. About twenty-five years ago, his imagination began saving unborn babies.

It started in casual conversation with his neighbor, Jack Bishop. Jack, an obstetrician, had just performed an emergency Cesarean section delivery. As it turned out, the mother who underwent the C-section was one of Lee's employees. So Lee was particularly inquisitive.

"Why do you have to wait so late to do a C-section?" Lee questioned. "Wouldn't it be better to know ahead of time if the baby is too big for the birth canal?"

"Well, of course it would," the doctor replied, "but we can't measure a fetus's head while still in the womb."

"I don't see why not," responded my unruffled friend. Lee had one of his ideas. A wonderful, beautiful, simple idea. He didn't generate it in the lab or with a high-powered computer program. His idea had a simple, quick birth. It was conceived in the womb of all good ideas: the imagination.

Lee's mind quickly returned to his service on U.S. submarines. Follow his thought pattern. Submarines are in water. Unborn babies are in water. Submarines use sonar to measure distance in the ocean's water. Sonar can measure distances in amniotic fluid.

Within about a minute's time, Lee Bryan developed an idea that would prevent a lot of emergency surgery and would help save a lot of unborn babies. His disclosure, entitled "A sonographic means for fetal head measurement,"[1] became one of the most important medical tools of our generation: the ultrasound.

When Lee tells the story, it sounds so simple that you're left wondering, "Why didn't somebody invent the ultrasound long before?"

For the same reason that the world was flat for so long—we were waiting for Galileo to imagine it round.

For the same reason that simple infections killed so easily—we were waiting for Sir Fleming to imagine that a mold could prevent it.

For the same reason it was dark so long—we were waiting for Edison to imagine a light bulb.

For the same reason we were on the ground so long—we were waiting for the Wrights to imagine their plane.

Nothing has come into existence until somebody imagined that it could.

How's your imagination? Here's a little game that will test your inventive qualities. Can you connect all the dots with four straight lines without picking up the pencil from the page and without backtracking?

You can find the solution at the end of this chapter, but please don't cheat. Get out a pencil and give it a try. Here's your only hint: Use your imagination.

Having difficulty? OK, here's another hint: Look beyond the boundaries. Try again.

Still stumped? OK, here's a dead giveaway: Imagine there is no box. Try again.

Still didn't get it? OK, go to the end of this chapter and check out the answer. But get back here quickly and read the rest of this chapter. You need it!

If you are like most, you had a problem with the test not because you weren't smart enough to figure it out. I'm sure you're very intelligent. But you assumed that you had to stay inside the box. Take note that I never told you to stay in the box. You decided for yourself that you could not draw outside the lines. If you stay inside the box, the puzzle is impossible. But as soon as you move beyond the preconceived boundaries, the impossible becomes possible.

Sadly, most of us adults have drawn boxes around our lives:

"My marriage can never be healed; it's too far gone." The first line of the box is drawn.

"My teenager will never quit rebelling." The second line of the box is drawn.

"I'll never be healthy again." The third line of the box is drawn.

"I'll never get out of debt." The fourth line of the box is drawn.

Your lines may be different. Some people make them thick; others make them long. But almost everyone I know has a box.

Except children.

Toddlers have no boxes around their lives. Their glorious imagination erases the boundaries of impossibility and replaces them with boundless life.

• Imagination is what empowers a parent's kiss to make a child's "boo-boo all better."

• Imagination is what makes peekaboo more fun for a child. Children can really believe that hands over eyes render the whole self invisible.

• Imagination is what makes little boys have more fun with toy trucks than construction workers have with real ones. It's what makes little girls love their dolls like they themselves are loved.

• Imagination is what makes pots, pans, and wooden spoons as splendid as any symphony's percussion.

• Imagination is what makes the cardboard box more fun than the hundred-dollar birthday present it contained.

• Imagination is what keeps a child on your lap to hear you tell the story "one more time."

Somewhere along the pathway to adulthood imagination fades. Boundaries darken. And, after a lifetime of hearing what you can't do, what you're forbidden to do, and what's impossible to do, your world may have grown very small.

If Lee Bryan is right about what separates humans from animals, God must love it when we are imaginative. That which makes us most human also makes us most like Him. We were created in His image. And the Lord is a God who loves to imagine the impossible. In eternity, He imagined time. In chaos, He imagined form. In darkness, He imagined light. In divinity, He imagined humanity. He is a God of infinite imagination.

So when He visited earth in the flesh, His imagination ran wild. He conceived of water becoming wine. He envisioned waves becoming a walkway. He pictured two fish becoming an all-you-can-eat buffet. He talked of camels traveling through needles' eyes, grown men being born again, and mountains jumping into lakes.

But Jesus was God in the flesh, you say. He was entitled to such miraculous, imaginative thoughts. Shouldn't we leave such grandiose thoughts to God's imaginative will and keep our feet firmly planted on the ground? No.

Jesus invited us to let our imaginations soar even beyond His: "I tell you the truth, anyone who has faith in me will do what I have been doing. He will do even greater things than these, because I am going to the Father" (John 14:12).

Surprisingly, *we* are the ones the Lord told to give orders to mountains: "Have faith in God," Jesus answered. "I tell you the truth, if anyone says to this mountain, 'Go, throw yourself into the sea,' and does not doubt in his heart but believes that what he says will happen, it will be done for him" (Mark 11:22–23).

The Lord isn't describing a small grassy hill sliding gently into the Sea of Galilee. The word Jesus used for *throw* is the same word the devil used to tempt Jesus to fling Himself from the temple. The disciples would have used the word daily to describe tossing their nets.

Jesus was speaking on the Mount of Olives. On a crystal clear day, from the crest of the Mount of Olives, you can see the Dead Sea lying, mirrorlike, in the desert. I bet the disciples turned and looked at it as Jesus spoke. But the Dead Sea is over fifteen miles away. To splash in the Dead Sea, the Mount of Olives would have to be uprooted and hurled through the air across a vast expanse of Judean wilderness.

Commentators are quick to remind us that "moving mountains" was a common idiom of the day used to describe the removal of difficulties. Truly, Jesus promises that there is no obstacle too great to be conquered through Him. But, still, I see no subtle, symbolic intention in Jesus' words. This is not a mountain slowly eroding. It is no quiet reassurance that time heals all wounds. This is no practical instruction on how to cope with life's problems.

This is a mountain with wings. This is a cosmic, "trans-desert" shot put of a mountainous rock into a distant, salty sea.

Jesus deliberately offended the rationality of His students. Everyone knows that mountains don't jump into oceans just because we tell them to. Every carpenter knows that you don't build big boats in the middle of a drought—except Noah. Every woman knows that you don't get pregnant when you're ninety—except Sarah. Every leader knows not to trap your people between the enemy and a sea—except Moses. Every soldier knows that you don't tumble walls with a trumpet—except Joshua. Every shepherd knows you don't knock down giants with a slingshot—except David. Every blind man knows that saliva and mud do not make eyes see—except the man who washed in the Pool of Siloam. Every father knows that dead daughters don't get up—except Jairus. Every prisoner knows that chains don't just fall off the wrists—except Peter. Every religious terrorist knows you don't suddenly love your enemy—except Paul. Every murderer knows that the victim's son doesn't go to the electric chair in his or her place—except the Christian.

Oswald Chambers said, "Imagination is the greatest gift God has given us."[2] In fact, it is essential. No one has come to Christ without imagination. At some gracious moment, perhaps gradually, perhaps suddenly, you imagined the impossible. You imagined that the eternal, unblemished God stooped to come into your dirty, time-trapped world. You imagined the unthinkable, that all the stupid mistakes, ugly stains, and haunting guilt could disappear. You imagined that this beautiful Lord was willing to be called every name under the sun, just so you could be called His son. You imagined a Creator willing to be killed by His own creatures, just to have their fellowship. Only a wild imagination can consider such love.

Imagination opened the door to eternity in Heaven. Why not let it open the door to more of Heaven on earth?

Years ago, Walter took his friend Arthur for a ride in the country. They bumped along unpaved roads, navigated through groves of trees, avoided grazing horses, and surveyed a large expanse of uninhabited land. After stopping the car, Walter's vivid imagination began pouring out incredible dreams for developing the property.

Walter pleaded with Arthur, "I can handle the main project myself. But it will take all my money. But the land bordering it, where we're standing now, will in just a couple of years be jammed with hotels and restaurants and convention halls to accommodate the people who will come to visit my development." He continued, "I want you to have the first chance at this surrounding acreage, because in the next five years it will increase in value several hundred times."

"What could I say?" Arthur later recounted. "I knew he was wrong. I knew that he had let this dream get the best of his common sense, so I mumbled something about a tight-money situation and promised that I would look into the whole thing a little later on."

"Later on will be too late," Walter tried to convince his friend. "You'd better move on it right now."

But Arthur didn't. And so Art Linkletter missed a chance to buy all the property surrounding Disneyland. He just couldn't imagine that his friend Walt Disney could pull it off.[3]

I'm sure Art and Walt remained friends. He didn't lose everything because he couldn't envision Walt Disney's park. He just missed out on the magic kingdom. And if you are a Christian with little imagination, God still loves you infinitely. You don't lose everything. You just miss out on a lot of His kingdom. Walt didn't love his friend less because Art turned him down. The Disneyland creator was just disappointed that Linkletter didn't comprehend all that was available to him. The Lord didn't love his disciples less because they couldn't envision the impossible. He was just disappointed that they weren't receiving all of the grace available to them. Jesus wasn't exhorting the disciples to do more. He was pleading with them to let God do more through them.

Do you remember what prompted Jesus' invitation to childhood? The disciples had asked, "Who is the greatest in the kingdom?" "Who has the most of Heaven?" It was a good question, and Jesus was glad for a chance to answer it. Children have the most of Heaven on earth because they have no boundaries around themselves or God.

Jesus invites you into a child's world where all things are possible. It is a chance to draw outside the lines. To live without a box. But it is not an invitation to a world of make-believe. It is an opportunity for belief to make the world. If you want to be a child again, erase your preconceived boundaries. Invite God to sanctify your imagination.[4] To plant a holy expectation in your heart. To birth a vision in your spirit.

Ask Him. After all, God uses His imagination more than anybody. If you'll ask the Lord to move mountains, He'll enjoy it even more than you. Imagine that.

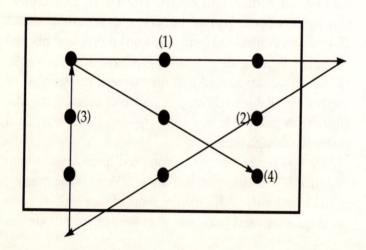

CHAPTER THIRTEEN

Short Battles, Quick Treaties

Childlike Forgiveness

"If you hold anything against anyone, forgive him, so that your Father in heaven may forgive you your sins."

MARK 11:25

Bob, my best childhood friend, lived across the street. It was good to have my best buddy's house only a Frisbee toss away. It was a short trip over. It was a short trip home. But best of all, it was a short trip back over. That allowed us the luxury of tromping home angry, vowing permanent separation, but returning within the hour.

It happened almost every day. Our day of play would begin quite merrily. "Hi, Bob. Whatcha want to do?"

"Let's play GI Joe," he might have suggested.

"Sounds great."

Out came the toy soldiers for combat. And the fun would begin. With imagination and love, my best friend and I would play with each other sweetly enough to make Mr. Rogers sing. But, inevitably, something would go

143

wrong. The toy combat would be replaced with real warfare.

"That's my GI Joe camouflage suit!" one might shout.

"No, it's not," the other would insist. "My mom gave me that for my birthday! Give it back!"

The tug of war began. "It's mine!"

"Is not!"

"Is too!"

R—I—I—P! GI Joe would then have only one camouflaged leg.

The momentary silence might be broken by a wail loud enough for the attending mom to hear, in hopes that she would scold the other. Or, more often, the battle would be waged right there and then. It was sudden, mouth-to-mouth combat.

"You ripped it! I can't believe it! I can't stand you!"

"I didn't rip it, you did! I hate your guts!"

"I'm leaving!"

"Good!"

And, with that, one or the other of us would march home, vowing never again to see, play, or associate with our former best buddy. But, once home, with no friend in the house, things could get boring pretty quickly. Besides, it's always more fun to play with the other guy's toys. So, it didn't take long. Maybe an hour. Maybe two hours, tops. The phone would ring.

"Hey, Alan, whatcha doing?"

"Nothing much."

"I've got a new Rockem Sockem Robot game. Want to come back over and try it?"

"I'll be right over!"

It was a short trip back. As children, we had open, intense frays. But the battles were short, and the treaties were quick. We had short memories (I actually can't remember the details of any skirmish Bob and I ever had). And we didn't even know the meaning of the word *grudge*.

How different for us "mature" adults. Our wars are long. Our treaties are slow. And it seems like miles back to one another. But the sources of our conflicts are just as stupid.

Consider the Pelford family. Mr. and Mrs. Pelford never had much. They somehow managed to raise three daughters and two sons on his farming income. But it was a day-to-day existence. There were no savings. After Mr. Pelford died, the family matriarch made it clear to the children that there was no inheritance coming. She was a little relieved. There would be no estate for the children to squabble over.

But Mrs. Pelford had a thick, golden wedding band. It was worth several hundred dollars. When the family gathered at the funeral home the night of their mother's death, one of the daughters exclaimed, "Where's Ma's wedding ring?"

It was gone, and each sibling claimed to have no idea where it was. But all were suspicious. No one said anything until after the funeral. When the family gathered at the eldest son's house for the dinner the church had provided, the youngest daughter dropped a bomb: "Not long before she died, Mama told me she wanted me to have her wedding ring."

She insisted that she hadn't taken the ring. But the other two daughters didn't believe her. They never spoke to her again. One brother said he didn't care if she took the ring or not. But he was so mad at the older sisters that he told them not to call him until they "grew up." The other brother believed his little sister was innocent and so was ostracized with her. Twenty-seven years later, when the oldest sister died, only one sibling came to the funeral.

Can a missing three-hundred-dollar wedding band really make a family miss a future together? Absolutely. But it doesn't have to be a wedding band.

> It might be as small as
> …your best friend's poorly timed comment about your hair.
> …your neighbor's puppy who ransacked your trash.
> Or it might be as large as
> …your husband's belittling remark at a party.
> …your boss's criticism that got you fired.

Any offense, minor or major, can become fuel for a feud. Anything can pull us apart. Only one thing can bring us back together. Anything can separate us. Only one act can reunite us.

Forgiveness.

As little children, it came so naturally, so easily, that we didn't know we were practicing the single most important biblical principle for relationships: "'In your anger do not sin': Do not let the sun go down while you are still angry, and do not give the devil a foothold" (Ephesians 4:26–27).

Forgiveness is critical because life has so much conflict. It was easy to confess my arguments with my childhood buddy Bob. It's harder to admit that I still have conflict almost every day with the people closest to me. It might be a disagreement with my wife, a disappointment with a parishioner, or a dispute with a stranger. But every day is tainted by wrongdoing. And every healthy human life will include anger.

God never said, "Don't be angry." Jesus Himself was unashamed of His anger. He was frustrated with the Pharisees and furious at the moneychangers. The Lord's entire earthly ministry was cloaked in conflict. But Jesus never let the sun go down on His anger. He didn't push it down in His soul and hide it. When He was frustrated, He showed it. But the Lord never brooded over His anger. He never stewed his frustration to the boiling point. Jesus was angry but did not sin. He faced conflict openly and never compromised righteousness. He rebuked wrongdoing consistently but held no grudge against those who wronged Him. Instead, His dying words were, "Father, forgive them, for they do not know what they are doing" (Luke 23:34).

Children embody Jesus' two primary exhortations about forgiveness: (1) Do it quickly; and (2) do it often.

As I am writing this chapter, we are vacationing at the beach. My wife's sister and her husband arrived today to join us. I wish you could have beheld the scene of their four-year-old Jake running full speed across the beach to embrace his two-year-old cousin, Bennett. I wish you could have heard the sound of their voices during their long hug. After being apart for an eternal two weeks, they declared their undying affection for each other.

"I've missed you."

"I've missed you too."

It was a scene that would have moistened the most macho eyes.

But you couldn't have wept for long. A toddler's day is a strange mix of sublime affection and horrific wrong-doing. For example, within a short afternoon

…Bennett kicked salt water on Jake.

…Jake stole Bennett's toy.

…Anna Katherine pushed Jake.

…Bennett ate Jake's grilled cheese sandwich.

…Jake stole the water hose from Anna Katherine.

...Bennett hosed Anna Katherine's freshly changed diaper with cold water.

Consider how much blatant wrongdoing three toddlers can accomplish in one afternoon. It was all there: covetousness, abuse (verbal and physical), theft, slander. But what is more amazing than the number of wrongs suffered is the number of pardons offered. Those three children went to bed with no shred of ill feeling toward one another.

How would you sleep if, in the course of a day, your best friend had yelled at you, your cousin had stolen your car, a neighbor's hose had flooded your basement, and a colleague had publicly scorned you?

Peter once asked Jesus, "'Lord, how many times shall I forgive my brother when he sins against me? Up to seven times?' Jesus answered, 'I tell you, not seven times, but seventy-seven times'" (Matthew 18:21–22). That's about what it took for those three toddlers to play together one afternoon on the beach. How much more forgiveness is required of us for a lifetime of conflict and wrongdoing in a sinful world?

Forgiveness is so crucial to the abundant life that Jesus attached a rare condition to it: "For if you forgive men when they sin against you, your heavenly Father will also forgive you. But if you do not forgive men their sins, your Father will not forgive your sins" (Matthew 6:14–15). What an awesome, terrifying teaching. Do you see its weighty uniqueness?

Jesus never taught, "Love others or else God will not love you." He didn't send out the disciples saying, "Get pagans saved, or else God won't save you." The Lord never declared, "Heal others, or God will not heal your diseases."

Forgiveness holds such unique importance to God that our whole prayer life hinges on our ability to forgive others: "Therefore I tell you, whatever you ask for in prayer, believe that you have received it, and it will be yours. And when you stand praying, if you hold anything against anyone, forgive him, so that your Father in heaven may forgive you your sins" (Mark 11:24–25).

Do not misunderstand the voice behind these urgent commands. This is no stingy God who is reluctant to forgive. This is the Lord whose mercy endures forever. This is the King of Kings who took on the form of a servant so He would be able to sympathize with your weaknesses. This is a Christ who wept over the spiritual blindness of Jerusalem. This a God who loves to forgive.

The urgency behind the heavenly voice finds root in the Father's great longing for His children. He wants you to have life more abundantly. He yearns for you to have the freedom of a toddler at play. But when you choose not to forgive, you choose to reject Christ's freedom. Simply put, it hurts you more than it hurts your enemy. When you choose to harbor hatred, you are the one who burns within. You are the one whose blood pressure rises. You are the one who loses sleep. You are the one whose stomach ulcerates.

Children refuse to live like that. So should we.

Why do children forgive so readily? The answer is not nearly as spiritual as you might think. Children forgive quickly and frequently for a rather selfish reason: They don't want to be lonely. They want to keep on playing. Children are more than willing to forgive in order to keep the fun. They'd much rather lose their pride than lose their buddy.

In a sad, stupid twist, many adults would rather lose their friends, their families, their fun than lose their pride by "giving in." Grudge keepers, wake up! You are the one paying the price. And it's not worth it. Even a two-year-old knows that.

As you've been reading this chapter, perhaps you've done a little personal inventory. Any grudges? Anybody you haven't forgiven? Before you say no, let's double-check your attitude toward the most unforgiven person in the world. In years of listening and counseling I've heard one person's wrongdoing mentioned more than any other. There is one human being that has earned a grudge from a countless throng of people. It doesn't seem fair, but over and over, this person can't seem to buy a lick of forgiveness. I'll tell you who the person is. But first, let me tell you about Jennifer.

Jennifer was always as sweet as sugar, but the flavor of

her kindness lasted longer. She brought us about seven different meals when our baby was born. But Jennifer had some quiet struggles with fear and self-esteem. She would meet with me often to talk, to pray. She loved God more deeply each day, but her anxieties did not subside. I prayed God would show me the source of her hidden fears so that I could help her find freedom. But years went by, and I didn't know. Until one day she told me.

"There's something I need to share with you," she said as her voice broke. "I don't think you'll like me anymore after I tell you this, but I think God wants me to tell you anyway."

I reminded her that her tears were OK and, once again, pledged my unconditional love.

She continued. "Twenty years ago, my husband and I conceived a child accidentally. We already had two girls, and times were so difficult. We didn't think we could bear the financial burden of a third. We were just trying to get off the ground."

Jennifer sobbed more deeply. I held her hand but dared not speak. I knew what was coming.

"I...we...really didn't want an abortion. But I rationalized. I made it all OK in my mind. And so I did it.

"But ever since that time, for twenty years, I've hated myself. Even though you've told me from the pulpit over and over that God loves me and wants to bless me, I couldn't believe it. Every time you would hug me at the end of church and say, 'God bless,' something inside of me screamed, 'No, God can't bless me. You don't know what I've done.' For twenty years, I haven't been able to accept the simplest of compliments."

Confidence began emerging in her voice.

"But last weekend, at the mountain retreat, something incredible happened while we were taking communion. I saw a T-shirt message: *Jesus died for you*. It was as if a warm blanket were wrapped around me. I felt an overwhelming peace touch me. It was as if a voice told me, 'Jennifer, I forgave you long ago. You just need to forgive yourself.'

"I realized," she said as a grin crept onto her face, "that God really loved me. That He really had forgiven me. I just hadn't forgiven myself. What I did twenty years ago was horrible. But I've realized that doesn't mean I'm a horrible person. In fact, I've got some pretty good qualities. I think I like myself pretty much. Ever since that communion experience, I have felt like a new person. I don't feel afraid anymore. I keep feeling this wonderful peace."

We thanked God, and I thanked her for sharing by adding, "Oh, by the way, Jennifer, I don't like you less for sharing this—I like you more."

What person is the object of the most grudges? Me. I don't mean just me, Alan Wright. I mean you. I mean ourselves. The person you may be slowest to forgive is yourself. So, when you make your list of "People to Forgive," you might need to put your name at the top.

You may not live across the street from your best friend like I did as a child, but you can shorten the distance in your relationships with childlike forgiveness. If you yearn for the freedom of childhood again, you'll have to quit trying to make people pay for their mistakes. They can't pay for their mistakes anymore than you can. Only Jesus can pay for sins. Aren't you glad He isn't holding a grudge against you?

CHAPTER FOURTEEN

"O-h-h-h Me"
Childlike Compassion

Mourn with those who mourn.

ROMANS 12:15

Not knowing what else to do, I stood motionless behind the grown son who held the hand of his dying father. It was my first church, my first months. I had never walked the road of cancer with a parishioner before. I was almost surprised at how deeply I cared for the man in the hospital bed. I didn't understand yet that God planned for me to love that bedridden man like Christ loved him. I didn't know yet that when God ordains a pastor, He provides the pastor's heart. So I just stood silently, surprised by the depth of my love, but disappointed by my feelings of pastoral ineptness.

Lester winced with pain. His medication at the time wasn't strong enough to mask his physical anguish. So his body constricted because of the pain emanating from his bones. He drew in a short breath and then exhaled slowly.

As he breathed outward, Lester rhythmically stretched out a moan, "O-h-h-h me." It was a pain-filled, mournful moan. But, at the same time, it possessed a compelling beauty. It was not just a cry of distress. It was a sigh of the soul. The more I listened, the more it sounded like a song rather than a moan.

"O-h-h-h me. O-h-h-h me."

The tender son leaned forward. I had been to seminary. I had been trained. But I watched this son carefully. His confident demeanor proved he knew how to care for his beloved father better than I. With a clasped hand and a hint of a smile, the son brought his face down close to his dad's.

Lester moaned again, "O-h-h-h me."

Then, what I never could have imagined to happen occurred. The son echoed back, "O-h-h-h me."

The white-haired patient moaned louder, "O-h-h-h me."

Again, the unfathomable echo came back from the son, "O-h-h-h me."

What was I beholding? Was such insensitivity possible? Could a son actually mock his dying father's moan?

I considered interrupting the son's echo of anguish. I contemplated pulling the man away from the bed to save his father from the humiliation. But oddly, Lester seemed comforted—not agitated—by his son's peculiar imitation. So, I stood silently and waited.

I was about to learn a holy lesson in compassion that I would never forget.

After watching this amazing father-son duet of moans for some time, I stepped out of the hospital room with the son. He explained.

When I first met this saintly, aging man, he was at home, not in the hospital. Though Lester's health was declining rapidly and his pain was increasing at the same rate, there was no place of healing like home. Lester was thankful for a fine hospital, but the hospital had no home-cooked meals, no view of Rose of Sharon Road, and no Wesley.

Wesley was Lester's two-year-old grandson. I knew this toddler to be a blond-haired barrel of fun who was bound to bring sunshine to the darkest of days. I had seen Lester's smile broaden when Wesley was around. I knew that Wesley's presence helped alleviate Lester's anguish. I knew how much he loved the little boy. But what Lester's son told me outside the hospital room that day touched my heart forever.

At home, as Lester's health worsened, he rarely walked. When he did, Lester supported himself with a walker. Each grueling step brought shooting pain. His walk was more of a shuffle, each slide of the foot an accomplishment. And with each foot forward, with each lift of the walker, Lester would exhale his usual moan: "O-h-h-h me." Step. "O-h-h-h me." Step.

One day, unprompted, little Wesley came alongside his shuffling, moaning grandfather. He placed his two-year-old hand at the base of Lester's walker, and with each painful step, Wesley "helped." With all his two-year-old strength, Wesley helped lift the walker upward and forward.

And following each of Lester's mournful moans, a two-year-old voice echoed back, "O-h-h-h me. O-h-h-h me."

Although I would like to have beheld the scene firsthand, I am more nourished by the picture I carry of it in my imagination. How different the man and the boy. There was more than seventy years between them. One had lived a lifetime; the other had hardly lived. One had bones brittle enough to make every trip down the hall risky; the other had bones supple enough to bounce on beds and fall off couches unharmed.

And yet, as Wesley echoed his grandfather's moan, how similar they were. Though the toddler was quicker, the size of their strides was about the same. Though Lester was a friendly talker, when in pain, his vocabulary was not much larger than little Wesley's. The old man and the little boy had a unique, beautiful connection as they walked and moaned together.

My seminary professors and pastoral mentors had taught me consistently, but never so powerfully or eloquently as that two-year-old boy, the most important pastoral lesson of all. When people are hurting their worst, our words need to be fewest. Aching saints do not need long-winded preachers or glib cheerleaders. They need someone who will come alongside them and, step by grueling step, acknowledge their pain. Hurting people need someone who, in the apostle Paul's words, will mourn with those who mourn.

In our frantic, hurried world, there are few who will slow their gait to the pace of the sick. Few who will risk exercising the literal meaning of compassion: "to feel with." But little children possess a rare empathy that attunes them to those who hurt.

And yet, little children do not waste a moment worrying about those who receive their care. After little Wesley helped his grandfather walk, I'm sure the little boy trotted off to play. Children teach us a lot about compassion by what they *don't* do.

Consider what two-year-old Wesley didn't do:

• Wesley didn't try to carry Lester. A little boy knows he can't carry a full-grown man. He wouldn't even think of trying. So he just walked alongside. He did what he could. No more, no less. Adults, on the other hand, often feel utterly responsible for the other's well-being. They not only care, but they try to carry the full weight of their loved one's burden. Such attempts inevitably fail. No one can take another's disease or bear the grief for him or her. We can care for others. Only God can carry them.

• Wesley felt no guilt. Little children don't condemn themselves for another's pain. My first experience in clinical pastoral education was excruciating. I would visit the hospital in the afternoon and come home with a headache and a big dose of guilt. "How can I just go on my happy, healthy way while there are people lying in those hospital beds suffering?" I would ask. The biggest challenge for me was not learning how to minister to the patients in the hospital but how to live with myself when I wasn't there. It finally dawned on me that my worry and guilt were doing those patients no good whatsoever. Little Wesley helped his grandfather walk, but then I'm sure he bounced off without a care in the world.

• Wesley didn't need to be needed. His care was pure. He had no personal need to moan. He wouldn't have felt bad about himself if Lester had asked someone else to help him walk. Adult caregivers, on the other hand, can get addicted to their caregiving. They can become as sick as the ones they are trying to help. To have compassion for a sick person does not mean you must become sick yourself. If you are going to pull someone out of quicksand, you'd best not jump in the quicksand yourself.

Little children are the best models of compassion because they care deeply but do not become consumed by the loved one's problem. Adults tend toward the extremes. They either show no care at all or become totally lost in the other's needs. They either never visit the nursing home or feel guilty every day they aren't there. Children show genuine love. But no child loses sleep at night feeling responsible for all the world's problems.

What makes a child's compassion so natural, so sweet?

Toddlers' hearts have not been calloused by the pain of the world. Their unscarred souls are still sensitive and soft. They are not scared to feel what others feel. They are not repulsed by another's pain.

The other day I foolishly tried to carry a glass-top table up the stairs by myself. As I lost control of it, the glass crashed around my falling body. There must have been angels protecting me. I suffered only one real cut. When our little boy discovered his dad's bleeding flesh wound on the knee, he wanted to kiss the "boo-boo" to make it better. I tried to persuade him that I needed no kiss. That didn't work. Bennett was not content to leave my knee unkissed. Though I was compelled to clean and dry the cut before the kiss, I allowed him to plant one right on the fresh wound.

I don't know that the flesh benefited from the kiss, but the soul beneath that flesh sure did. Is there a greater healing balm than a love that looks beyond our ugly exteriors? Is there a touch that better restores our wounds than the touch of genuine compassion?

Who else but a child, I wondered, would kiss an oozing wound?

Who else but Christ?

- Who else would touch a leper's open sore?
- Who else would take a prostitute's hand?
- Who else would drink a Samaritan's water?
- Who else would lend the touch of his garment to an unclean, bleeding woman?
- Who else would wash his betrayer's feet?

Who else but a God of compassion. Jesus relinquished His heavenly throne to come alongside us. John said it this way: "The Word became flesh and made his dwelling among us" (John 1:14). It means literally, He "pitched His tent" among us. He suffered in the ways we suffer. He was tempted in the ways we are tempted. Therefore, the author of Hebrews insists, "We do not have a high priest who is unable to sympathize with our weaknesses" (Hebrews 4:15). The prophecy proved true: "He was despised and rejected by men, a man of sorrows, and familiar with suffering" (Isaiah 53:3).

The caring Christ is so different from the dying creature. He dwells in eternity. We are trapped in time. His world is infinite. Ours is limited by height, width, and depth. He is spirit. We are flesh. He is all light. The world is all dark. But compassion compels Him to come alongside.

He wanted to feel what we feel. And, oh, how He did. He felt the pangs of a hungry stomach, the pain of desertion, and the power of the ungodly. Jesus listened to the call of the devil, the crash of the storms, and the crack of the whip. He sweated. He wept. He ached.

And one dark Friday, they lifted His body to a cross. There, hanging on the cursed tree, Jesus felt the collective pain of the world. There, alone, He felt the alienation that sin had brought upon all humanity. There, as He slowly suffocated, the Savior managed a loud moan, "Eloi, Eloi, lama sabachthani?" (Mark 15:34). Mark translated the Aramaic words, "My God, my God, why have you forsaken me?" But they might as well have been "O-h-h-h me."

CHAPTER FIFTEEN

Never a Loser
Childlike Celebration

Rejoice with those who rejoice.

ROMANS 12:15

My plane was late. The list of arrivals and departures on the screen told me so. But I didn't need the video monitor to discover the wearisome delay. The information was also readily available on the faces of the bored travelers sitting in the terminal. With each impatient glance at the clock, the sad passengers displayed their frustration.

But one passenger didn't seem to mind the delay at all. In fact, he was celebrating. He was smiling, laughing, and squealing with glee. Occasionally, he would fall on the floor and laugh out loud.

The jubilant traveler looked to be about four years old. It was probably his first time to fly. I wondered if he'd ever been in an airport terminal before. From the huge terminal windows, the little boy had a wide-eyed view of the runway. Every takeoff was cause for celebration. Every landing, a reason to rejoice. With any jet's arrival or departure, the playful child shouted, "Hooray!" threw his hands into the air, and danced a little jig. Then, amused with himself, the tot would squeal with delight and fall on the floor in drunken hilarity.

My adult cotravelers and I smiled at the boy's antics. Though no one joined his party, we all silently, secretly, longed for the boy's heart. We craved his freedom. Inwardly, we know we were not created for drudgery but for celebration. We would give anything for life to be so much fun again. We desperately want to be lifted from a life of boredom and frustration into a life of expectancy and jubilation. But life's blows have blinded us. We've seen so many failures that we hardly notice the victories. We're so concerned about our personal setbacks that we miss the triumphs all around us. We are so consumed with our own puny agendas that we miss the grand victory celebration of the cosmos.

The child and the adults were in the same airport, waiting on the same plane, looking out the same windows. The child's circumstances were no different from the adults'. But he had a fundamentally different presupposition. The little boy assumed that *every* plane's landing was a cause for joy. As far as we adults were concerned, there would be only one reason for rejoicing: the arrival of *our* plane.

The little boy had no more reason to celebrate than we

did. He just celebrated more. All little children are that way.

Our two-year-old loves basketball. Sometimes we watch a "whoosh ball" game on TV together. I enjoy it, but he has twice the fun I do. I have fun only when *my* team scores. Bennett celebrates when *either* team makes a basket.

Bennett has it made. He gets to celebrate no matter what. He's never a loser. Always a winner.

Unknowingly, little children are living out a simple biblical principle: "Rejoice with those who rejoice" (Romans 12:15).

Why limit your joy to your own occasional triumphs? Imagine how much better life would be if you could celebrate your coworker's promotion as much as your own. Wouldn't life be grand if you could enjoy your neighbor's greener grass as much as if it were in your own yard?

Little children don't have more to celebrate. They just celebrate more things. They don't win more often than adults. They just act like winners more often. It leaves me wondering: Which comes first in life, the victory or the celebration?

I married a winner. Literally.

Anyone who knows my wife would tell you the same thing. At almost any given time, Anne is celebrating some recent win.

The year before our wedding, Anne and I visited her Uncle Stanley and Aunt Joella in Los Angeles. I investigated a seminary there, and we spent a week of fun in the California sun. The day before we were to fly back home, we walked from the Farmers Market to the nearby CBS studios to inquire about watching a TV production. It was just a last-minute lark. We all thought it would be fun to see a sitcom or a game show being filmed.

Usually people get tickets by writing for them well in advance. But, as it turned out, there were a few seats available to see *The Price Is Right* later that day. We decided it would be a fun outing. Besides, with Anne's "luck," she'd probably be the first person called down and would probably win it all.

She was, and she did.

In a strange way, I wasn't even surprised when Johnny Olson made his exuberant call, "Anne, come on down. You're the first contestant on *The New Price Is Right.*"

The first item up for bid was a trip for two to the French Quarter of New Orleans. She bid slightly higher than the other low bids, and Bob Barker announced the actual retail price and said, "Anne, you have won. Step on stage, and let me show you what you might win next."

Anne pranced up on the stage, placed a peck on Barker's cheek, and turned her eyes toward side stage as the famous emcee declared with glee, "Anne, look what you can win—a new car!" The curtains parted to reveal a sparkling Oldsmobile. Anne made guesses at the car's price playing a game aptly named Lucky Seven.

No problem. She won the car.

Later in the show, Anne competed against other contestants by spinning a big wheel. Whoever came closest to the value of a dollar on the wheel won a place in the final showcase. Anne won the spin of the wheel.

Her showcase included an ultralight airplane; a trip for two to Jackson Hole, Wyoming; and a brass bed. When Anne made her bid, the audience gasped with horror, thinking it was way off the mark. But when Bob Barker unveiled the showcase's value, Anne's bid was only $150 off the actual price.

By the show's end, she was over $20,000 richer!

But Anne's winnings did not begin or end with *The Price Is Right*. She still finds money unexpectedly. She spots four-leaf clovers with only a casual glance toward the lawn.

When there's a raffle, people want Anne to pick the number out of the hat for them. If there are door prizes to be given away, people try to sit near her at the dinner table. If there's a bingo game, people want her card.

She meets famous people and visits fascinating places. Where there are two or three gathered, Anne is in their midst telling about some hilarious or exotic experience she has recently had.

Most worldlings call her lucky. Most saints call her

blessed. But, however you put it, my wife is a winner.

With all this in mind, my mother recently asked an interesting question: "Does Anne really have more exciting things happen to her, or does she just tell it better?" Mom smiled as she asked it, but the question was really quite poignant. Does Anne really win more than most, or does she just have a winning attitude? Do some people have a lot more to rejoice about than others, or do they just rejoice more often? Do some people have more cause for celebration in life, or do they just live in such a way as to cause more celebrations?

I think I know the answer to Mom's question. But to explain, I need to let you in on a little secret about *The Price Is Right.*

The contestants aren't randomly selected. There was no drawing from a hat that put Anne on contestants' row. It was no lucky number that put her name in front of Johnny Olson's microphone. She was handpicked for a reason.

An hour before the show, the producer interviewed every member of the viewing audience. It was very brief and quite informal. But it was all the producer needed. Just two or three questions as we walked by. "Where are you from? What brings you to Los Angeles? What do you do back home?" And as the producer asked the questions, an assistant stood nearby quietly taking notes.

The man in front of me was so nervous he could hardly

speak. His lip quivered, his knees shook—and the producer quickly dismissed him. I got even less attention. "What do you do?" I was asked. "I'm in the ministry…" I started to say. I hardly let the words out of my mouth before they were saying, "Next please."

Anne was next. When she told the producer her home state, he playfully mimicked her southern drawl, "No-orrth Car-a'lain-a." As usual, Anne's enthusiasm showed itself in her bright face. Her smile had no pretense; her chuckle was authentic. And within thirty seconds, the producer knew that he wanted Anne on the show. I'm sure after years of picking contestants, the producer had learned what kind of person everyone likes to see win.

And it *was* fun watching Anne win! She didn't go berserk or leap wildly about the stage after her victories. But, as always, she displayed an unguarded, childlike love of life. Her celebration was not held in check, nor was it overdone. Her squeals of delight and hugs of Bob Barker were equally genuine. Her celebratory spirit was winsome and contagious. The audience was glad she won and, I'm sure, so was the producer.

We still pull out the videotape of the show and watch it for fun every now and then. But it's even more fun just to hear Anne tell it.

"Does Anne really have more things to celebrate, or does she just celebrate more?" The answer is both. She really is blessed in astounding ways. She really does have exciting experiences. She really does have a lot of victories. But she invites all that excitement with her celebratory attitude. She's not a winner because she's had a lot of victories. She's had a lot of victories because she has a winner's heart.

Joy seeks a rejoicing heart. Songs seek a willing singer. Victory seeks a ready winner.

That's the way the kingdom of God is, Jesus said. "I tell you that to everyone who has, more will be given, but as for the one who has nothing, even what he has will be taken away" (Luke 19:26). The ones who celebrate most will have more to celebrate.

If your life motto is, "I have the world's worst luck," then you probably will. You will always expect the worst, look for the worst, and the little bit of good that does happen you will soon forget. If, on the other hand, your life motto is, "Boy, I am always blessed," you'll look for the blessings, remember the blessings, and even when life is tough, still be blessed.

God loves celebrations. He instituted regular festivals for His children just so the Israelites would not forget to celebrate. The Lord told Moses that the Passover "is a day you are to commemorate; for the generations to come you shall celebrate it as a festival to the LORD—a lasting ordinance" (Exodus 12:14). Jesus was celebrating the Passover when He told His disciples, "This is my body given for you; do this in remembrance of me" (Luke 22:19).

We don't wait for some great pinnacle in our Christian walk before we celebrate the Lord's Supper. In fact, it's when we walk through the valley that we most need to celebrate the sacrament. Likewise, we mustn't wait for our life circumstances to become perfect before we rejoice. Over and over, the Scriptures tell us to rejoice regardless of life's condition:

- "My soul will boast in the LORD; let the afflicted hear and rejoice" (Psalm 34:2).
- "Though the fig tree does not bud and there are no grapes on the vines, though the olive crop fails and the fields produce no food, though there are no sheep in the pen and no cattle in the stalls, yet I will rejoice in the LORD, I will be joyful in God my Savior" (Habakkuk 3:17–18).
- "We...rejoice in our sufferings" (Romans 5:2).
- "Rejoice in the Lord always. I will say it again: Rejoice!" (Philippians 4:4).
- "But rejoice that you participate in the sufferings of Christ" (1 Peter 4:13).

This command to rejoice is no scriptural candy coating of life's pain. Rather, it is God's reminder that no earthly trouble dethrones the King of Kings. It is God's reminder that a great victory has been won, and you are on the winning team. To "rejoice in the Lord always" doesn't mean you're supposed to be happy about sicknesses and rebellious teenagers. Instead, it means that even when there are sicknesses and rebellious teenagers, you have plenty in God to celebrate.

Two thousand years ago the Messiah won big. Death, danger, disease, the devil—everything that contaminates life—stood impotently by as Christ was proclaimed champion. Easter is the Lord's victory shout. Heaven is one eternal victory celebration.

You'll have to wait until you get to Heaven to have a struggle-free life. But you don't have to wait to start celebrating. You can join Heaven's victory party any time you're ready.

Observe the little children. They find something to celebrate in every facet of life. And so, life itself is a celebration. Don't limit your victory celebrations to your own puny successes. The whole universe is ablaze with God's winning glory.

Every sunrise proves the Artist is still painting. Every dogwood blossom proves the Creator is still creating. Every birth proves the Potter is still spinning His wheel. Every eternal longing proves the Groom is still courting His bride. Every peaceful moment proves the Comforter is still comforting. Every weeping sinner proves the Father is still running to meet His children.

If you want a chance at childhood again, you'll have to learn to celebrate someone else's victory. Thankfully, you don't have to look far to find a victor. Open your eyes.

Look heavenward. Your Father has won it all. And when you're His child, you're welcomed to the celebration. Rejoice! You can never be a loser.

CHAPTER SIXTEEN

Letting Loose
Childlike Praise

David...danced before the LORD with all his might.

2 SAMUEL 6:14

One of my colleagues has a special parishioner who requests the same hymn every week. The parishioner is amazingly persistent. Week after week, he beseeches the minister, "Pastor, when are we going to sing 'Holy, Holy, Holy'?"

Week after week, the pastor reassures him, "Soon. I promise we'll sing it sometime soon."

My pastor friend is not irritated by the request. "Holy, Holy, Holy" is a great hymn. And the parishioner making the weekly request is a little boy with Down syndrome. His name is Josh.

Josh may be confused about a lot of things, but he knows exactly where his favorite hymn is in the old, red Presbyterian hymnbook. It's number eleven. The bulletin reads, "No. 11 Holy, Holy, Holy." So that's what Josh calls it. "No 11." Every Sunday morning my pastor friend can count on Josh pleading, "Pastor, can we sing 'No 11 Holy, Holy, Holy' today?"

One Sunday morning, the pastor had selected number eleven as the opening hymn. He didn't wait for Josh to come pleading. Instead, the pastor found Josh.

"Josh, do you know what we are going to sing today?" my friend asked enthusiastically.

"What?" Josh asked as his eyes widened.

"Josh," the pastor continued, "guess what we are going to sing today!"

"What? What?"

"Josh, today, we are going to sing 'Holy, Holy, Holy'!"

Josh paused as if not knowing how to respond. His eyes widened further, his mouth dropped open, and a great, victorious grin stretched across his face. Josh raised a triumphant fist into the air. Then, yanking his arm downward in victory, Josh simply hollered, "Y-e-s!"

Josh's theology is unsophisticated. His testimony is an unpredictable blend of Jesus and Indiana Jones. And when he sings No. 11, "Holy, Holy, Holy," he misses a lot of words and almost all the notes. But no finely tuned, red-robed, hundred-voice choir could make a more joyful noise. No pipe organ or cathedral orchestra could issue finer praise than Josh's hungry, unabashed, all-consuming "Y-e-s!"

No pride hinders his praise. No approval poll quenches

his ardor. No need for sophistication slows his singing.

Josh's shout of joy defines praise more plainly than the keenest theologian's pen. Praise is the unhindered celebration of a holy, holy, holy God. No one could argue with the uninhibited praise of a little boy with Down syndrome. But when it's an adult who gets ecstatic over God's holy presence, people raise their eyebrows.

When the elders of Israel anointed David king, the Jebusites occupied Jerusalem. The little city, hardly twelve acres big, thought itself invincible. Their steep city walls atop two canyons and their secret underground water tunnel gave them confidence against invaders. But they weren't just confident. The Jebusites were cocky.

When David's men marched to attack the town, the Jebusites laughed in the king of Israel's face: "You will not get in here; even the blind and the lame can ward you off" (2 Samuel 5:6). The Jebusites shouldn't have laughed.

Scripture doesn't describe how David conquered Jerusalem that day. He may have invaded through the secret tunnel. The Bible tells us just this: (1) The city of the Jebusites became the "City of David" (v. 9); (2) David's reign spread because God was with him (v. 10).

It wasn't the first time that David had seen God conquer the invincible. He had seen a taunting Philistine giant fall to his shepherd boy's stone and sling (1 Samuel 17:49).

He had seen the Amalekites crumble before him (1 Samuel 30:17). He would soon see the fierce Philistines struck down (2 Samuel 5:25).

When you see God win your most threatening battles, what is left to do but praise Him? When you see God go before you in the tough times, you want God to go before you in the soft times.

So when David took his throne in Jerusalem, he wanted the King of the universe to be enthroned before him. David wanted God's glory to go into the city with him. So he arranged a parade of celebration to bring the ark of the covenant into Jerusalem. The ark symbolized the holy presence of the living God. It was too holy to touch. All of Israel received a shocking reminder of this truth when Uzzah presumptuously touched the ark and died. The ark can be carried—but God cannot be controlled.

The Lord's purity is unfathomable to dirty human minds. His strength is unsearchable for frail human flesh. His throne is too high for nearsighted mortal eyes to behold. The holiness of God requires not our understanding but our awe. And when this holy God willingly enters the fellowship of His people, there is no adequate response but praise:

So David went down and brought up the ark of God from the house of Obed-Edom to the City of David with rejoicing. When those who were carrying the ark of the LORD had taken six steps, he sac-

rificed a bull and a fattened calf. David, wearing a
linen ephod, danced before the LORD with all his
might, while he and the entire house of Israel
brought up the ark of the LORD with shouts and
the sound of trumpets. (2 Samuel 6:12–15)

King David danced. And it was no Arthur Murray
waltz. The Hebrew words literally mean "he whirled
around and around." Trumpet blasts and shouts of joy
filled the air. David leapt and spun about like a child who
could not contain his excitement.

Can a toddler sit still while a parade marches by? Can
a little boy stay calm while opening presents on Christmas
morning?

How then can a Christian fall asleep while praying?
How can a pew sitter yawn while singing "Crown Him
with Many Crowns"?

Praise is not praise unless it remembers the victory
God has won. Worship is not worship unless it knows that
God is present. For David, the victory was fresh. God's
presence was tangible. For many Christians, the Easter
victory seems distant; God's presence, forgotten.

David's victory celebration was not emotionalism. His
faith didn't rest on his feelings. But when he felt the joy of
the Lord, he wasn't ashamed to show it. I like what my
childhood preacher always said: "I don't want to go on
feelings, but I sure don't mind feeling what I'm going on."

David felt what he was going on. He felt the grace and power of God. He felt the wonder of His presence. And he couldn't contain it. The king let loose.

He shed his royal robe. The cumbersome garment weighed him down. It hindered his whirling dance. So David shed his kingly raiment. And as he laid down his robe, he laid down his pride.

David was left wearing a linen ephod. The simple smock was the attire of a priest—one who worships. And so, as he danced, the king was no longer above his people, he was among them. He was not over them, he was with them.

The Hebrew peasant girls celebrated, but Israel's first lady watched with disdain:

> As the ark of the LORD was entering the City of David, Michal daughter of Saul watched from a window. And when she saw King David leaping and dancing before the LORD, she despised him in her heart.... When David returned home to bless his household, Michal daughter of Saul came out to meet him and said, "How the king of Israel has distinguished himself today, disrobing in the sight of the slave girls of his servants as any vulgar fellow would!" (2 Samuel 6:16–20)

Michal could not join in the unguarded praise. Michal, the daughter of a king, thought she knew how a king should act. She supposed that losing pride meant losing position. She did not understand that though David shed his royal garments, he did not shed his royal office. The outer trappings of royalty or religion do not make a man, nor do they move God. She did not understand that God is not concerned with a king's robe. The Lord cares about a king's heart.

So David's wife stayed perched in her lofty window where she could hold onto her pride. She kept her dignity. But she missed the dance. The Bible says that Michal despised David. But the text does not say that David despised Michal. Nor are we told that God disdained her.

Instead, we are given only a sad parenthesis: "And Michal daughter of Saul had no children to the day of her death" (2 Samuel 6:23).

David, the dancer, saw the fruit of his reign increase. Michal, the dignified one, was left barren.

I'm a Presbyterian. I've been trained to worship decently and in order. I've been taught to be suspicious of emotionalism and excess. I've been educated about the havoc of fanaticism and the dangers of phoniness. An out-of-control, religious flake is the last thing I want to be.

Well, almost the last thing.

The last thing I want to be is barren. Outwardly dignified—but inwardly dead. Having the form of religion but missing the freedom of real worship. Having the robe of respect without the mantle of genuine anointing.

Having the dignity of Michal's window but missing the joyous freedom of David's dance.

Every major revival in the history of Christianity has found root in people who let go of pride and utterly abandoned themselves unto the worship of God. Whether it's the apostles in the upper room, Presbyterians in the Great Awakening, Pentecostals on Asuza Street, Promise Keepers in the Georgia Dome, or parishioners in Toronto, all real renewal happens among those who prefer praise over pride.

You cannot lift up yourself and God at the same time. You cannot revere God while wanting people to revere you. Real praise is so consumed with God's goodness that it is unconcerned with the world's opinions.

The Bible never mentions Michal again. But David is called a man "after [God's] own heart" (Acts 13:22).

A thousand years later, David's great, great, great...grandson was born in David's hometown of Bethlehem. This child, too, was a king who would be despised by the proud but loved by the humble. In his years on earth, King Jesus shed his heavenly robe for an earthly ephod. In His own way, as the Shaker hymn tells it, the Lord danced. His life and ministry were an unabashed, unhindered celebration of God's reign on earth. He healed, He delivered, He empowered. But He did not do so in the normal manner. The leaders of His day did not think His behavior fitting for a Messiah. They watched in derision from their lofty positions of authority. And, in disgust, they tried to kill His celebration. But they could not.

God's dance goes on. The angels are still blowing their trumpets. The heavenly band is still playing. And the dance floor is still open.

If you want the joyous freedom of childhood again, you don't necessarily have to whirl around in church. But you do have to put praise before pride.

And maybe you could at least try this. Find an old Presbyterian hymnbook. Turn to number eleven. Put one hand in the air. Then jerk your fist downward and shout, " Y-e-s!"

CHAPTER SEVENTEEN

How to Waste Time

Childlike Priorities, Part I

Very early...Jesus...left the house and went off to a solitary place, where he prayed.

MARK 1:35

It takes us forever to get out of the house and into the car anymore. It didn't use to be so tough. I remember a serene time in which my wife and I would just glide out the door and slide comfortably into the automobile. Now, with a toddler in the house, it takes an act of Congress just to run a simple errand.

We call it "getting on the treadmill." It's a lot of exercise that gets us nowhere. But, unlike the cardiologist's test, our toddler treadmill tests the heart's spiritual capacity. People had predicted to me that things would take a lot longer with a child around. I assumed they were referring to the bottles to be heated, pacifiers to be sterilized, diaper bags to be packed, and little lunches to be prepared. I presumed the parental forecasters meant that life would be slower because of all the new *things* that had to be done. I found out it's not the *things* that slow the parent down. It's the child.

When it comes to getting things ready, we are a well-oiled machine. My wife is an especially efficient mom. She can stock a diaper bag with a sippy cup, extra apple juice, a buffet of lunch items, extra diapers, baby wipes, pacifiers (in little baggies for cleanliness), ample toddler reading material, a few toys, an emergency change of clothes, and a surprise snack faster than a stock car pit crew can get a racer back on the track. It's not the *things* that get us on the treadmill; it's the boy himself.

Every parent has experienced it. His shoes are on...now his shoes are off. "Where did his sock go?" He wants to read *Winnie the Pooh* "one more time." "OK, you can bring the book with you." He needs to putt a golf ball—now the golf ball is under the couch. Oh, there's a tumble. "Come here, where's the boo-boo? Let me kiss it." He needs a long hug. "Where is his other sock?"

The treadmill phenomenon applies to more than just getting out of the house. The same principle works for getting out of the bathtub, the sandbox, or the toy store. Children are just slow. They don't intentionally contrive cruel schemes to slow their parents down. And they aren't really procrastinating, either. They just aren't in a hurry.

"Inefficient," a businessperson might call it. "Dilly-dallying," a parent might say. No matter how you phrase it, children waste time.

Adults, on the other hand, are stingy with it. We learned, along the path to "maturity," that personal success is summarized by accomplishment, and self-worth is measured by productivity. We learned to cram as much activity into a day as possible. Over and over we were told to "hurry up," and we learned that "time is money." So we make sure never to waste a minute.

Jesus must not have known those adages. He sure didn't live by them.

Think about how Jesus used His time. His days on earth were numbered. And the number was low. He lived thirty-three years but didn't start His ministry until He was thirty. Why didn't He get going earlier? As a twelve-year-old kid, He amazed people at the temple with His knowledge. Why didn't He get into an accelerated gifted-and-talented track at school and graduate ahead of schedule? He could have begun His ministry by age twenty or twenty-five. Today's ministers get three years of seminary training in preparation for thirty years of ministry. Why did Jesus have to spend thirty years preparing for only three years of ministry?

And regarding His extremely short period of ministry, most business consultants would seriously question His time-management skills. Let's see how Jesus scored on some of the usual time-management tips for professionals:

Time-Management Principle #1: Don't just make a list of things to do—schedule your appointments and tasks in your daily calendar.

No Jesus DayTimer scroll was discovered in the Qumran caves. In fact, though He came in the fullness of time, Jesus evidently scheduled nothing. The Gospel accounts of His ministry show the Messiah moving from place to place, event to event, without any apparent preplanning. With the huge crowds that followed Him, even the disciples questioned Jesus' apparent lack of forethought. Two fish and five loaves can hardly qualify for a potluck. What church administrator would plan a huge fellowship dinner but fail to call the caterer? And in rereading the important events surrounding His crucifixion, the only bit of planning I noticed was Jesus' directive to two disciples to go into the village ahead for a colt. That could hardly be called advance planning.

Can you imagine the president of the United States scheduling a major appearance but not choosing a mode of transportation until the day of the event? The president has every minute of his day scheduled long in advance. The King of Kings had no calendar.

Time-Management Principle #2: Avoid interruptions.

Interruptions, the time managers teach us, are the professional's worst enemy. They get us sidetracked and prevent us from doing other more important tasks. If an "intruder" comes into your office uninvited, stand up. Be polite, but don't allow the interrupter to sit down. Use your secretary, if necessary, to buzz you. See the person to the door. But don't get trapped by an unexpected, unwanted meddler.

Jesus would have flunked this principle outright. He not only tolerated interruptions, He seemed to enjoy them. He let Himself get cornered by a Pharisee at night. In Capernaum, a paralytic was let down through the roof in the middle of an important sermon. Instead of scolding the man or quickly getting back to His topic, Jesus forgave the man, healed the man, and opened up a controversy by doing so. A blind beggar stopped Him on the street, a short tax collector distracted Him from atop a sycamore tree, and a Samaritan woman kept Him at the well a long time. Twice Jesus was on His way to heal someone but, because He was interrupted, didn't get there until the sick person had died!

Time-Management Principle #3: Avoid unproductive time.

Watch out for unproductive periods, time-management gurus warn. Don't squander your time in activities that don't produce tangible results. Avoid unproductive meetings. Keep focused and alert.

Jesus inaugurated His ministry with forty days of isolation. All He seemed to accomplish during those desert days was to get Himself mightily tempted and so weak that angels had to minister to Him. Then, early in His ministry, He frittered away a day at a wedding party. And though there were scores of sick people who needed healing and thousands of distraught people who needed counseling, Jesus often withdrew to do nothing but pray. In the middle of a potentially devastating storm at sea, Jesus took a nap!

Jesus' use of time would have exasperated most church professionals today. His view of time bears more similarity to my two-year-old's view than it does to that of most of today's successful pastors. Jesus had so little time. Three short years. Yet He acted like He had all the time in the world. He was never once frustrated by feelings of unproductivity. The Lord never regretted the use of His time. The Messiah accomplished every single bit of ministry that He wanted to accomplish. But He never hurried. A lot of people never got to speak to Him. But if you had come to Him with a problem, He would have never looked at His watch. He wouldn't have hustled you away in order to make His next appointment.

Jesus was surrounded by a busy Roman world and by busy religious leaders. But nowhere in the Gospels does our Lord seem busy.

Aren't you tired of feeling so busy? I sure am.

As exasperating as the toddler treadmill can be, I yearn

for the freedom of such an unhurried life. Don't misunderstand, I want to be active. I want to accomplish great things for Christ. I just don't want to be frantic in doing it. Can you imagine the joy of accomplishing everything you want to accomplish in life but never feeling busy while you do it?

Jesus invites us to such an unhurried life. Considering how children and Jesus both view time, I am reminded of two essential principles of life and ministry.

1. Important things over urgent things

The Gospels don't record the names of all the people who didn't get healed or touched by Jesus because He was off in a solitary place praying. Even though He was God in the flesh, Jesus could not be in all places at all times. He could not see everyone or touch everyone. But He never once felt stressed about that limitation. Likewise, toddlers do not feel guilty about not marking off enough "to do" items. Jesus didn't do everything. He simply chose the important things. Little children are naturals at that as well.

Adults spend so much time trying to please people, trying to answer the unanswerable, and worrying about the unknown, that there is little time left for life. When our child was seven weeks old, I held him after a particularly worrisome day and sought his help to soothe my troubled mind. Our conversation went something like this:

Important Matters

Since you're just from heaven,
Won't you lend me your ears?
How'd God make the world,
Was it in days or in years?

Tell me, Bennett, the former or the latter?
I just want to know what you think of the matter.
And when it comes to the end,
Are you pre-mill or post-?
Can you tell me His time,
Can you even come close?

Lend me your ears, Son, and quit all that chatter,
Your father's confused; what do you think of the
    matter?

What preacher was right?
Which scholar most smart?
Was it Calvin or Luther?
Was it Tillich or Barth?

I see you're hungry, so you want to get fatter;
Forget about milk; what do you think of the matter?

What about your creed, Boy,
Which one of them wins?

Do we say Spirit or Ghost,
Trespasses or sins?

I see that yawn, those eyelids that batter,
Forget about sleep, Son; what do you think of the
    matter?

In seven weeks on earth,
Have you not learned a thing?
You've just come from Heaven,
But what wisdom do you bring?

I see your smile—don't think that it flatters.
Tell me, Little Boy, what do you think of these mat-
    ters?

What's that...?
The answer is clear?
Lean down...?
Yes, I'll give you my ear.

Dad, here's my thought over all of these matters,
Let's just keep playing, 'cause none of it matters.

The only occasion I remember Jesus openly com-
mending a person for time use was during His visit to the
home of Martha and Mary. Martha was working frantically

to get dinner ready while Mary "sat at the Lord's feet listening to what he said" (Luke 10:39). Busy, productive Martha became so frustrated with her sister that she dared question the Christ, "Lord, don't you care that my sister has left me to do the work by myself? Tell her to help me!" (v. 40). Martha might as well have shouted, "Lord, don't let my sister waste so much time!"

Jesus' response didn't beat around the bush. He told Martha what really matters most in life. "Martha, Martha," the Lord answered, "you are worried and upset about many things, but only one thing is needed. Mary has chosen what is better, and it will not be taken away from her" (vv. 41–42).

What matters most? Listening to Jesus. Drinking in His Word. Marveling at His wisdom. Putting aside all distractions. Going deep in prayer. Bowing at the authority of His commands. Warming at the familiarity of His voice. Relaxing under the sound of His promises.

You must sit at His feet. How else will you know how to spend the rest of the hours of your day? Who else knows enough and loves you enough to teach you what's important for your life? The TV will mislead you. Advertisers will brainwash you. Corporations will consume you. Even church affairs can distract you.

Listening to the Lord takes a lot of time. There were untold urgent needs all around Jesus, but He withdrew often, just to be with His Father. We need time with the

Father even more. Glancing at a verse and hastening on will not do it. We must meditate upon His Word—turning it over and over in our souls. We must give the seed time to germinate. We must water it daily. It takes a lot of time. And prayer takes time. Prayer is not, "Hi, God. How are you doing? Thanks for a nice day today. Bless me tomorrow. Good night. Amen." Real prayer longs to discover the heart of God. Real prayer treasures most highly the secret wisdom of the Creator.

Sit at Jesus' feet. The world might call it a waste. Jesus calls it worship.

2. People over programs

Jesus never wrote a book, never held an office, and never organized or implemented a church program. Instead, He spent most of His time hanging around twelve men. Jesus poured His time into people. He valued relationships above everything. That's the way children are.

No matter how enticing a toy or how inviting an activity, a toddler wants to be at Mommy's feet. Take away all the toys, videos, and games, but leave Mommy, and a toddler is fine. Take away Mommy, but leave all the toys, videos, and games, and the toddler is in tears. Children remind us that the cultivation of love relationships is the best use of our limited earthly time.

How foolish of you, Dad, to spend so much time building the swing set that there is no time to swing with your daughter. How tragic, Mom, to spend so much time making money for your boy's education that you've no time to offer him the best education of all: a parent's wisdom.

Song for a Fifth Child

Mother, O mother, come shake out your cloth!
Empty the dustpan, poison the moth,
Hang out the washing and butter the bread,
Sew on a button and make up a bed.
Where is the mother whose house is so shocking?
She's up in the nursery, blissfully rocking!

Oh, I've grown as shiftless as Little Boy Blue
(Lullaby, rockaby, lullaby loo).
Dishes are waiting and bills are past due
(Pat-a-cake, darling, and peek, peekaboo).
The shopping's not done and there's nothing for stew
And out in the yard there's a hullabaloo
But I'm playing Kanga and this is my Roo.
Look! Aren't her eyes the most wonderful hue?
(Lullaby, rockabye, lullaby loo.)

Oh, cleaning and scrubbing will wait till tomorrow,
But children grow up, as I've learned to my sorrow.

So quiet down, cobwebs. Dust, go to sleep.
I'm rocking my baby. Babies don't keep.[1]
                    (Ruth Hulbert Hamilton)

Little children naturally gravitate toward people, not programs. They are not dazzled by superorganized birthday parties. They just hope their best friends are there. Children could care less how much they produce as long as they are with the ones they love.

No one has ever come to his or her deathbed and declared, "I wish I had developed more programs, produced more, and made more money." Everyday, people come to the close of their years with the dying regret, "Oh, how I wish I had spent more time with those I love."

It still amazes me how our two-year-old can totally stall his efficient parents and turn the smallest tasks into day-long ventures. His unhurried pace can be exasperating. But what frustrates me more is my own lack of such serenity. I pray daily for God to protect him from the driven, frantic pace of the world. I'd much rather he keep the unhurried heart of a child doing only what pleases God, rather than gain all the world's accolades and lose his unrushed life.

Do you want to be a child again? It seems odd. But maybe you need to waste more time. Just waste it on Jesus.

CHAPTER EIGHTEEN

How to Waste Money
Childlike Priorities, Part II

"Why wasn't this perfume sold and the money given to the poor? It was worth a year's wages."

JOHN 12:5

When my nephew Christopher was little, he tried his hand at a little bartering with some older neighborhood boys. Young Christopher returned home excited because he took away more bills than when he started, plus a comic book. Imagine his mother's exasperation when she discovered her little boy had traded his crisp five-dollar bill for two ones and a thirty-nine-cent comic book.

Not only are children often blind to the dollar's value, but they are also prone to be impulse buyers. Unattended, a youngster might spill his whole piggy bank for ten bags of candy-coated popcorn or for thirty-two tries on the same video game.

But worse than their ignorance about the value of a hard-earned dollar and their impulse buying is the toddler's treatment of possessions. They don't guard their stuff and protect it like adults do. Little boys don't wash and buff their toy cars. Instead, they push them until the wheels fall off. Little girls will rub the fur off their teddy bears and squeeze the stuffing out of their dolls.

Toddlers don't preserve their belongings. They waste them. I can't convince our two-year-old to turn off his plastic radio or his new toy flashlight to conserve battery life. Bennett gives no thought to the way the salty ocean water rusts his toy trucks. And he'll gladly throw his most prized possessions into a deep lake just for the joy of watching the treasures sink.

Children are so wasteful. They squeeze the toothpaste from the middle and don't turn the water off while brushing. They like to eat only the four juicy inner bites of their grilled cheese sandwiches. At birthday time, they lick the icing off and then leave the rest of the cake on its paper Barney plate. And what child won't happily dump out a whole box of cereal just for the prize at the bottom?

As little children, we didn't live by the principle of scarcity. We lived by the principle of plenty. If we wasted a little, so what? We felt confident that the provisions would not run dry.

But, along the path to adulthood, we became "economical." We were told over and over, "Money doesn't grow on trees" and "A penny saved is a penny earned." Over the years, we learned a simple rule of thumb: Don't spend any unnecessary money.

It didn't mean that we had to become stingy, although a lot of us did. Instead, it meant don't ever blow a dollar. Don't let a dollar slip through your fingers unless you get an equally valuable product in exchange. Make sure you always get a good return on your investment. Whatever you do, don't pour money down the drain.

Wasteful children can be exasperating. Wasteful adults are unacceptable.

Maybe that's why the Messiah was rejected by so many.

In the eyes of today's financiers, Jesus had little money sense. It's true, He was surrounded mainly by men who lived hand to mouth. And, sadly, his accountant, Judas, wasn't on the up and up. But there's no one to blame for Jesus' attitude about money except the Lord Himself. He just didn't operate according to the same principles the world does. Evidently no one had taught him, "Money doesn't grow on trees." He never worried about money and always acted as if there would be plenty of provisions.

Far from the common sense principle of never blowing a dollar, Jesus once told a wealthy man to give away all his possessions. He even commended a poor person for giving the little she had. Several times, in parables, Jesus commended men who blew money. In one account, a manager squandered his boss's money by canceling debts that several clients owed the employer. Jesus commended the manager's savvy for winning friends in such a strange manner. In another story, Jesus applauded a landowner who gave employees more pay than they deserved. And in the familiar parable of the talents, the practical saver was scorned and the servants who gambled it all in various investments were praised.

But the incident that surely raised the most eyebrows is recorded in John 12. Jesus, having accepted a dinner invitation, arrived as usual at the home of his friends. He had been to Mary, Martha, and Lazarus's house before. Scripture records at least two other visits. He probably was over for dinner often. As far as anyone knew, He would be back for many more. It was customary for a servant to wash the guests' feet with water. But Jesus' feet were bathed not by a servant. They were washed by one of His hosts.

> A dinner was given in Jesus' honor. Martha served, while Lazarus was among those reclining at the table with him. Then Mary took about a pint of pure nard, an expensive perfume; she poured it on Jesus' feet and wiped his feet with her hair. And the house was filled with the fragrance. (John 12:2–3)

Judas was the only disciple who dared to express his outrage. The greedy liar didn't really care about the needy, but he was smart enough to know what everyone was thinking. So he said it out loud. "But one of his disciples, Judas Iscariot, who was later to betray him, objected,

'Why wasn't this perfume sold and the money given to the poor? It was worth a year's wages'" (vv. 4–5).

A year's wages! That bottle of perfume was worth about $30,000 by today's standards. Imagine what you could do with that kind of money! How would you have felt watching $30,000 poured into the dirt? How would you have felt watching the dust become mud? Thirty thousand dollars—that's nearly $2,000 per ounce.

Did Mary at least pour it slowly? About three good drops make an ounce—$2,000 into the dirt. Put yourself there. Behold it with your own eyes.

Drip. Drip. Drip. There goes the first ounce.... Could have sponsored eight children in a Third World country for a year. Would have meant food, education, exposure to Christ.

Drip. Drip. Drip. There goes the second ounce.... Is she really going to pour it all out? Could have run an outreach Vacation Bible School for a hundred kids. Wonder how many would have accepted Christ?

Drip. Drip. Drip. There goes the third ounce.... Another $2,000 becoming mud. Could have kept the community shelter open for a month with those three drops.

Drip. Drip. Drip. There goes the fourth ounce.... Could have been Christmas for twenty orphans who won't get presents this year.

Drip. Drip. Drip. Is Jesus going to let this waste continue?

He sure is.

In fact, Jesus not only allowed it, He commended Mary for it: "'Leave her alone,' Jesus replied. 'It was intended that she should save this perfume for the day of my burial. You will always have the poor among you, but you will not always have me'"(vv. 7–8).

Mary's extravagant gesture was not without cause. The episode makes a little more sense when you remember the miracle Jesus had performed not long before. Lazarus had fallen sick. When Jesus delayed, Lazarus died. Seeing the deep anguish that Mary felt over the loss of her brother, Jesus, too, was deeply moved. With never-before-seen power, the majestic Messiah shouted Lazarus out of his tomb. Lazarus's final resting place was not final. Jesus' word was final.

That's why Mary poured $30,000 on the Savior's feet. The last time she had seen Jesus, her brother had been lying in the grave. This time, Lazarus was reclining at the table. The last time Jesus visited, there had been tears of woe. This time there were tears of joy.

The $30,000 was more than worth it, of course.

Some friends of ours lost their precious two-year-old in a freak recreation accident last week. We wept with them at the grave beside the miniature coffin. Caskets should never have to be so small. I'd gladly plunk down $30,000 this minute if it would bring that little boy back to his mom and dad. How much would those parents be willing to spend? Thirty million dollars would feel like a small sum. If you're talking clothes or boats or cars, $30,000 is a lot. But it's nothing when you're talking about a person's life.

Even Judas would have had to admit that it was worth $30,000 to bring Lazarus back to life.

But Jesus had already brought the dead man back. Lazarus was already alive again. The miracle had already been accomplished. No payment was required. Even if Mary had not given the perfume, Lazarus would have remained alive and well. Suppose Mary had given the perfume, then in response to her gift, Jesus had restored Lazarus's life. No one would have questioned it. It would have been called a good investment. A good return on the dollar.

But this $30,000 gesture was not necessary. It was a waste. And Jesus loved every ounce of it.

He loved it because the sweet scent of His freshly anointed feet reminded Him of the whole reason for His coming. He loved it because here was a woman who was captured by the gospel. Don't miss this. It's so simple. But it's the most important thing you can know about God. Jesus gave Lazarus his life back because He loved him—not because someone paid Him. He breathed new life into the dead man because His compassion ran so deep—not because either Lazarus or his sister had earned it.

Jesus gave Lazarus's life back to him because grace always goes first.

"This is love: not that we loved God, but that he loved us and sent his Son as an atoning sacrifice for our sins" (1 John 4:10).

Grace not only goes first, it goes where it is not deserved. If you are a Christian, it's not because you paid God to save you. It's because He loved you too much to let you stay dead.

"But God demonstrates his own love for us in this: While we were still sinners, Christ died for us" (Romans 5:8).

The world calls Mary's expenditure a waste because it earned no return. Jesus loved her gift precisely because it didn't.

Mary spilled her perfume out of sheer, unbridled adoration of the Messiah. She knew that her anointing was by no means extravagant compared to the anointing the Father had already poured out upon His Son. The bottle was merely a symbol of her own heart. The perfume, her own soul. She was pouring out her own inexpressible affection to her Savior.

As she let down her hair, she violated every norm for a Jewish woman of her day. She might have been despised more for her extravagant immodesty than for her expensive gift. But she gave no thought to either. I imagine she did not let the oil out slowly. It probably was not a drip-by-drip drama. I think she let it out ever so freely. It flowed out and downward like the river of gratitude in her own spirit. As the precious oil pooled at His feet, her only regret was that there was not more to spill.

And as the fragrance of gratitude filled the room, so did the pleasure of the Lord. As the aroma of adoration lingered, so did Christ. For though our small offerings and little acts of righteousness do not manipulate the Sovereign Lord, God does inhabit the praise of His people. Jesus wanted no fellowship with religious people who thought His love could be bought. But Christ would spend all day with a grateful sinner.

The next time you see a child "wasting" something precious, think about Mary and her perfume. And think about Jesus.

I wonder sometimes what the angels said to one another as they watched the Son of God put on human skin and subject Himself to torture. As they watched the King of Kings reduced to a naked, bleeding outcast, I wonder if they thought it…I wonder if some angel dared to say it…"What a waste."

Out of unfathomable affection, God gave a far more extravagant gift than Mary did. He sent His Anointed One to be broken open with nails and a spear, spilled out, and poured upon you and me.

I still can't understand why God would "waste" His life on the likes of me. It leaves me wondering, "What can I waste on Him?"

Jesus' invitation to childhood again is certainly not an invitation to poor stewardship or stupid financial management. It *is* important that children learn the value of a hard-earned dollar, and they *should* learn to take care of their toys. But oh, that children could keep the truth in their hearts: Money is only money, and things are meant to be used not hoarded. And oh, that we adults would remember that sometimes money is best spent on the totally unnecessary. A wife knows that a gift of a useful vacuum cleaner from her husband means something different from a gift of a useless sapphire ring. A husband knows the difference between a backrub that precedes a request and a massage that just says, "I love you." And don't think God is fooled. He knows the difference between Judas and Mary.

It sounds unusual, I know. But if you want to be a child again, you need to learn to waste your money. Just waste it on God.

CHAPTER NINETEEN

Take This Job and Love It!
Childlike Work

Whatever you do, work at it with all your heart, as working for the Lord, not for men.

COLOSSIANS 3:23

Children don't know what a hard day's work is. Until we adults tell them.

One afternoon not long ago we were baby-sitting our three-year-old nephew and one-year-old niece. Wanting their parents to return home to extra happy children, we filled the afternoon with fun activities. What could a toddler enjoy better than an afternoon of Popsicles, Winnie the Pooh videos, and kickball? We were proud of how sweetly the little cousins played together and looked forward to giving a happy, no-tears report about a fun afternoon.

But late in the afternoon, I ruined it all. I decided to mow the lawn.

While the children were playing happily inside with my wife, I decided to slip out and cut the grass before dusk. I had put off the dreaded chore all week. It was getting dark, and the meteorologist predicted rain the next day. If I procrastinated another day, I'd have to machete the lawn before mowing it. So I cranked up the push mower and began the unpleasant task, dripping in the late summer, North Carolina humidity.

When I mow the lawn, I have one thought on my mind: finishing. With that consuming focus, I didn't notice that my nephew had come out of the house. Little Jake was standing on the sidewalk crying out to me. I shut off the lawn mower to hear him.

"Uncle Alan, I want to mow the lawn with you."

I smiled, crouched down, and told my little buddy that only Uncle Alan could use the big mower and reassured him I'd be done shortly.

I resumed mowing. But after two more passes over the lawn, Jake was still standing there. His call was louder. He was pleading, begging, bargaining with me. In an attempt to appease him, I fetched a broom and asked him to "help" by sweeping the sidewalk.

It didn't work. As I cut two more swaths of grass, Jake laid down his broom, broke into tears, and sobbed. He wept with his whole heart at full volume. When I went to comfort him, he was inconsolable.

"I just wanted to help you mow the lawn, Uncle Alan," Jake cried out repeatedly. "I just wanted to help you."

As my attempts at consolation failed (along with various bribes), I thought to myself, *"What is wrong with this picture?"*

I thought about asking him, "Let me get this straight. Inside the house there are toys and playmates. In the backyard there is a swing set and slide. But you would rather push a heavy mower through shin-high grass in the July sun? You would rather be shoving this mower, with ragweed flying up your nose and yellow jackets nipping at your ankles?

"You're mixed up," I was tempted to say. "Mowing isn't fun. It's work. Don't you know the difference between work and play?"

But there was no need to ask. Jake's desire to mow the lawn was no different from the desires of any other young child. All toddlers beg to do the chores their parents dread. They don't just covet mowing. They want to rake, bake, and vacuum. My two-year-old considers it a great treat when he gets to help me take out the trash or pull weeds.

Thankfully, I held my tongue. Jake will be told to hate work soon enough. The whole world will teach him. He'll learn it from commuters' faces on Monday morning. He'll learn that when people say, "Thank God it's Friday," they're not really thanking the Lord but cursing their work. He'll hear people gripe about their jobs and will listen to country musicians sing about taking this job and shoving it.

So I just hugged little Jake and longed for a heart that

draws no boundaries between work and play. And I thought how great would a country be if its people worked with the joy of a child at play? How much better built would our buildings be if all the workers had the fervor of a child with Lego blocks? How soon would we discover a cure for cancer if every science student worked with the determination of a child with a jigsaw puzzle? How much less crime would we have if, as a child, everyone received as much love and attention as a toddler's baby doll?

I realized that Jake isn't mixed up about work. I am.

During a recent stay at a nice hotel, I was excited about the sophisticated exercise room boasting five different stepping machines. But it perturbed me that the elevator was broken and I had to take the stairs to get there. Likewise, people who go to the mall to get out of the house and walk will, nonetheless, spend fifteen minutes driving around the parking lot to get a space twenty feet closer to the entrance.

It's strange. Children can't wait to grow up and do the work of adults. Adults can't wait to retire and quit doing the work they once longed to do. Children spend their early years pretending to be firemen and nurses and truck drivers. Real firemen and nurses and truck drivers spend their adulthood thinking about collecting a pension and getting out of the rat race.

It makes you wonder. Where did we go wrong? When

did work start feeling so much like work?

You don't have to turn far in your Bible to find the answer. Work was cursed at the same time that every other curse entered the world: when Adam and Eve disobeyed God's simple command.

The woman brought a curse upon the fruitfulness of her womb: "I will greatly increase your pains in childbearing; with pain you will give birth to children" (Genesis 3:16).

The man brought a curse upon the fruitfulness of his hands: "Cursed is the ground because of you; through painful toil you will eat of it all the days of your life. It will produce thorns and thistles for you, and you will eat the plants of the field. By the sweat of your brow you will eat your food" (vv. 17–19).

If the above verses were all you read, you might think that work was a curse that God put upon humanity. Such thinking leads to the conclusion that man and woman's disobedience made God so angry that he invented work to oppress the creatures.

That's the way most people view work. As a curse. An oppressive necessity. Hence, getting off work is better than going to work. Friday is better than Monday. If work is a curse, then we should do only what is necessary to get what we want in return.

I once imagined that Adam and Eve just lounged around their lush garden before the Fall. No weeds. No in-season or out-of-season. No planting or harvesting. No pits in their apricots. No worms in their corn. Surely paradise was like a great cruise-ship getaway. Plenty of sweets, swimming pools, and smorgasbords.

But, oddly, in Adam and Eve's paradise there is no mention of midnight buffets or freshly prepared salad bars. There are no waiters serving the couple frosty drinks with little, floating umbrellas. It appears that Adam and Eve had to pluck their own fruit. They had to crack their own coconuts, peel their own bananas, and squeeze their own orange juice. God was not dropping food in their mouths like a mother bird to her wide-beaked babies.

There was work to do before the Fall. Adam had a vocation before he ate his apple. The Scripture says it plainly: "The LORD God took the man and put him in the Garden of Eden *to work it and take care of it*" (Genesis 2:15).

The Hebrew word for *work* means "to till" the ground. Adam didn't have a gas-powered tiller or tractor. He probably didn't have much of a hoe. God put the man in the garden to work it with his hands. Adam had a strenuous, time-consuming job. And he loved it—until he sinned.

Adam had changed. There was tilling of soil before the Fall and tilling of soil after it. But Adam's attitude changed totally. The Hebrew word for *painful toil* usually refers to emotional pain, not physical pain. All of a sudden, work felt like work.

What began as a vocation to be enjoyed became a job

to get done. The calling that was a gift and blessing to Adam suddenly felt like a tyrannical task hanging over him. He perspired before the Fall, but now he noticed the sweat. His hands were in the dirt before the sin, but now they felt dirty.

Like everything else, sin made work a selfish endeavor. Adam quit working as unto the Lord and started working as unto himself. After sin, there was no more caring for the earth. It became all about *taking* from the earth. Before, the soil in his hands was a reminder of God's magnificent provision. Afterwards, it was only a necessary means of gain.

How do you see your work? A calling, or a paycheck? How do you view your chores? An opportunity to bless your family, or an aggravating necessity?

Author Sue Bender lived a hurried, chaotic life. Around five o'clock each morning, she began her busy, driven days with an ambitious "Things to Do" list. Maybe you can identify with her when she writes, "I valued accomplishments. I valued being special. I valued results."[1]

But, feeling unsatisfied with her busy life, Sue Bender decided to do something quite unusual. She moved in with an Amish family in Brimfield, Iowa.

The Amish are a simple people stereotyped for their shunning of electricity and automobiles. They are recognized by their simple black-and-white attire and their horse-and-buggy travel. While their religious separatism may be misguided in some ways, the Amish people remind America of a time when life was a lot slower and the line between work and play a lot fuzzier.

The busy, fast-paced author was surprised to watch the Amish women at work, cooking, canning, and cleaning. "No one rushed," Bender observed. "Each step was done with care. The women moved through the day unhurried. There was no rushing to finish so they could get on to the 'important things.' For them, it was all important."[2]

And she watched Eli, the father of the family, work the fields.

"Caring for the land, every day, is my way to be close to God. His land must be honored," she heard Eli say. And watching the Amish farm their land, Bender learned:

> Their intention is to make things grow and do work that is useful. I couldn't say exactly what the difference is, but I felt a difference. They work to work. Their work time isn't spent "in order to do something else"—to have free time on weekends, go to a restaurant, or save for a vacation or retirement. They do not expect to find satisfaction in that vague "something out there" but in the daily mastery of whatever they are doing.[3]

In summary, Bender noted the Amish do not just value the product of their work. They also value the process.

That's what little children do.

Children don't build sandcastles in order to take pictures of them or in hopes of winning a cash award. They build sandcastles just for the pleasure of the process. My little nephew Jake didn't want to mow the lawn so he could stand back and observe a manicured yard. He just wanted the pleasure of pushing the mower.

Adults value the results. Children value the means. Before the Fall, Adam valued the process of tilling the soil. Afterwards, he mainly valued the product of tilling the soil.

For a chance at childhood again, we must learn to value the process of work as well as the product. Our work, like our lives, must be redeemed.

Work needn't be drudgery. The curse can be broken.

Paul, one of the hardest working men in history, had a simple prescription: "Whatever you do, work at it with all your heart, as working for the Lord, not for men, since you know that you will receive an inheritance from the Lord as a reward. It is the Lord Christ you are serving" (Colossians 3:23–24).

You don't wash dishes for the family. You wash them for the Lord. When you change a diaper, you don't just serve your child, you serve Christ. You don't sell real estate for a commission, you sell it for the Lord. You don't argue a case for a jury's decision, you argue for the Lord.

Imagine if your work became God-centered rather than me-centered. Imagine if the process became as important as the product. Wouldn't it take the pressure off? Wouldn't it bring back the fun?

There was work in paradise before the Fall. There surely will be work in Heaven. But you'll forget to call it "work." In even the most challenging tasks, you'll feel like a child at play. Who knows, I may beg an angel to let me take a turn mowing some celestial lawn.

But while you're waiting to get to work in Heaven, why not get a little more of Heaven in your work now? Ask God to change your attitude about your work. Ask Him to help you work like a child. It may not happen overnight, but be patient. God is still *working* on you. And God loves His work.

CHAPTER TWENTY

"Because I Said So, That's Why"

Childlike Obedience

Be careful to obey so that it may go well with you.

When my brother Mark was a tot, he saw a sight he'd never seen before at the beach. An intriguing, transparent, puffed-up blob rested motionless on the sand. He figured it was an unusual balloon. So Mark thoughtlessly poked the odd sphere with his toe.

It wasn't a balloon. It was a beached jellyfish. With its potent poison, the seemingly innocent blob shot pain through the child's toe that sent him screaming.

Though they look similar, there's a big difference between balloons and jellyfish. Mark found out the hard way.

Thirty years later, Anne and I are walking with our tot on the beach. Bennett sees a sight he's never seen before. Another beached blob that looks like a most interesting balloon. It looks irresistibly fun to a toddler. If allowed,

Bennett probably would not only poke it with his toe but also pick it up and squeeze it.

But Bennett doesn't touch the dangerous creature for one reason. We tell him no.

Being told no is frustrating to a toddler. There's no way to convince a two-year-old that a motionless, transparent puff on the beach can sting like fire. He simply doesn't have the capacity to comprehend it on his own.

We tell him that if he touches the jellyfish, it will hurt. But we make no attempt to explain why it will hurt. We offer no lecture on marine biology. There's no point in teaching him that the jellyfish is a living organism whose sting remains viable even while beached. There's no use in describing how it floats with dangerous tentacles dangling beneath its body. It would be silly to spend time differentiating it from the similar Portuguese Man of War.

All the marine biology books in the world could not convince Bennett to leave the blob alone.

So we must lay down the law: "No Touching Jellyfish."

Of course, we lay down the law about countless other things as well. A few of the laws are proclaimed for our benefit as much as his. For example, "No Throwing Food from the Highchair" saves us from crouching down after every meal to pick up mashed bananas. But most of the laws are decrees designed solely for Bennett's protection. And, like the jellyfish prohibition, most of the laws are incomprehensible to his two-year-old mind. For example:

• "Thou Shalt Not Eat Only Chocolate for Dinner." One day he'll understand about nutrition, vitamins, and high-fat foods. But for now it's just a law.

• "Thou Shalt Not Run Around with a Whole Golf Ball in Thy Mouth." One day he'll understand about tracheas, choking, and CPR. But for now it's just a law.

• "Thou Shalt Not Bang on Thy Daddy's Computer." One day he'll understand about delete keys, deadlines, and irretrievable documents. But for now it's just a law.

• "Thou Shalt Not Hurl Thy Shoes into the Back of Thy Mommy's Head in the Car." One day he'll understand about concentration, dangerous driving conditions, and airbags. But for now it's just a law.

Though the above decrees may make you smile, real law is no laughing matter. I once read of a little girl who thought her parents were just playing a game when they said, "Come here." Upon hearing the command, the two-year-old would laugh, squeal, and run in the opposite direction.

One day the family was standing in the front yard as the little girl wandered toward the road. Seeing a car coming, the mother screamed to her daughter, "Come here!" The unknowing child laughed, squealed, and ran to her death.

We can't wait until our children understand our reasons before we draw boundaries. And when they ask, "Why,

Mommy, why?" sometimes the only sufficient answer is, "Because I told you so, that's why." Or did you ever hear this one? "Because I am the mommy. When you grow up and become the mommy, then you can make the rules."

Children aren't in charge of the world. They don't know best. No matter how much fuss they make, children cannot make their own rules and live.

If you want to become a child again, you may feel frustrated too. It's hard to admit that you don't know what is best. It's hard to accept that you can't make your own rules and live.

If you ask God why you must obey His rules, the Lord's answer will sound strangely reminiscent of what your parents used to tell you: "You must obey my laws and be careful to follow my decrees. I am the LORD your God. Keep my decrees and laws, for the man who obeys them will live by them. I am the LORD" (Leviticus 18:4–5).

Why must we obey God? Because He said so, that's why.

There's no point in questioning His decrees—they are final. There's no reason to hope His rules will change—they are eternal.

- A jellyfish is never a balloon.
- Adultery is never love.
- Gossip is never compassion.
- A homosexual relationship is never a marriage.
- A grudge is never righteous indignation.

A permissive parent is an unloving parent. What father would watch his child move toward a jellyfish and not issue a prohibition? What sort of Heavenly Father would know how broad is the road to destruction and not proclaim a warning?

The law of God is proof that He wants only the best for His children: "Hear, O Israel, and be careful to obey so that it may go well with you and that you may increase greatly in a land flowing with milk and honey, just as the LORD, the God of your fathers, promised you" (Deuteronomy 6:3).

The Lord's prohibitions are designed to make life "go well" for you. His boundaries are meant to bring "increase" to your life.

Dr. James Dobson's best-selling book *Dare to Discipline* confronted the trend toward permissive parenting that many psychologists promoted in the 1970s. When asked if children really want to have limits set on their behavior, Dobson explained by way of illustration.

During the early days of the progressive education movement, one enthusiastic theorist decided to take down the chain-link fence that surrounded the nursery schoolyard. He thought the children would feel more freedom of movement without that visible barrier surrounding them. When the fence was removed, however, the boys and girls huddled near the center of the play yard. Not only did they not wander away, they didn't even venture to the edge of the grounds.... There is security in defined limits.[1]

Likewise, the law of God is not designed to confine you but to expand you. The Lord does not desire to fence you in. He wants to take you to the edges.

"My son, do not make light of the Lord's discipline, and do not lose heart when he rebukes you, because the Lord disciplines those he loves, and he punishes everyone he accepts as a son." Endure hardship as discipline; God is treating you as sons. For what son is not disciplined by his father? If you are not disciplined...you are illegitimate children and not true sons. No discipline seems pleasant at the time, but painful. Later on, however, it produces a harvest of righteousness and peace for those who have been trained by it. (Hebrews 12:5–8, 11)

When I was a kid, I preferred playing at my friend Bob's house because I could get away with more. The rules were pretty much the same. But his mother would never discipline me in the same way my mom would.

Parents discipline their own children, not others'.

No child should fling a fork across a restaurant. It

could poke out an eye, or worse. If I saw someone else's child fling a fork, I would duck and murmur under my breath. But I would not attempt to discipline someone else's child. If it were my own child tossing the silverware, I would provide some prompt negative reinforcement. The law is universal: "No Flinging Forks." But the discipline is personal.

Likewise, God's laws apply to all. But His discipline is reserved for His children. God loves the world enough to reveal His rules. He loves His children so much that He disciplines them to obey the rules.

Several years ago we had a large family gathering for dinner out. The seafood restaurant was crowded. The service was lousy. We were already on edge, but with delayed food delivery and hungry stomachs, our fuses became even shorter.

Our three-year-old niece was particularly squirmy that evening. As little Sarah's mischief grew, her father issued a solemn warning: "Sarah, if you don't calm down, I'm going to take you outside and spank you."

Sarah calmed down temporarily. But time elapsed. The waitress made another false promise about our food being nearly ready. Our patience grew thinner. And Sarah started acting up again.

Her dad spoke to her again in his most serious tone: "Sarah, do you remember what I told you?"

The blond-haired three-year-old stopped to think

about her father's question. Just enough time had elapsed since the previous caution that she could not remember the exact wording of her father's earlier warning. She thought hard about it for a long moment.

Then, as if a light bulb went on, she spoke up by quoting a little song she had learned at church. In an innocent three-year-old voice she earnestly asked, "Do not be overcome by evil?"

"No," her father reminded her, "that's not exactly what I said. But it's close."

How amazing! Her father had threatened a spanking. But Sarah associated it with overcoming evil. Her three-year-old mind had already connected a father's discipline with a child's victory over evil.

That's the purpose of God's discipline for His children—that we not be overcome by evil. The Heavenly Father is not content to simply issue heavenly decrees. He personally disciplines each of His children to guide them into victorious living. The Book of Proverbs repeats the refrain: Fools despise the Lord's discipline, but the wise welcome His correction.

You've probably never mistaken a jellyfish for a balloon. But I'm sure that like me, you've been stung by your sin many times. There are a lot of spiritual jellyfish in the world. A lustful video. A white lie. A silent grudge. Seemingly innocent, they invite a curious poke but administer a painful poison. You can't poke at sin without getting stung.

There is a better way. It is the way all children must go. Admit that your Father knows best. Submit to His rules. Welcome His discipline.

> He who ignores discipline comes to poverty and shame, but whoever heeds correction is honored. (Proverbs 13:18)

CHAPTER TWENTY-ONE

The Fundamentals of Napping
Childlike Sabbath

"Remember the Sabbath day by keeping it holy."

EXODUS 20:8

Parents of toddlers, please don't drool when I tell you this. All children are different. Some need more; some need less. But our two-year-old takes a three-hour nap every day.

Only a parent can understand the magnificence of such a siesta. And a mother appreciates the gift the most. Three free hours. Three deliciously vacant hours to feel like a person again. Three hours for a mom to have an adult conversation or read a book. Even certain household chores are strangely satisfying when there is no toddler fastened to your leg.

But as important as the afternoon nap is for the parent, it is more important for the child. Without a nap, the most docile boys and girls can become wild, alien creatures. The sweetest little children can become incorrigible

226

grumps. Such "napless wonders" (our family term) soon turn their parents into aliens and grumps as well.

I don't understand why children need so much rest. But when they don't get it, some important physiological balance seems to go haywire. You cannot please napless wonders. No amount of toys and snacks can satisfy the transformed creatures. You cannot communicate properly with them. No bribe is good enough. No threat scary enough. Overtired children will whine, complain, and cry over anything.

The only thing worse than a napless wonder is two or more napless wonders in close proximity. The unrested children lose whatever dab of social skill they've achieved and plummet to a zero tolerance level. One parishioner discovered the epitome of sibling squabbling. Her tired, restless children bickered over minutiae in the backseat of the car until one child finally cried out, "Mom, Sammy's breathing my air!"

The fundamental importance of a nap is this: No child can go all day without stopping, at least for a while.

Neither can an adult.

We can go without naps. But we can't go without snoozing. God deliberately designed us to require sleep. Adam slept before the Fall (remember what he was doing when God borrowed his rib?). And the Second Adam, who never "fell," slept also (remember what Christ was doing during the storm at sea?).

Of course, the Lord could have designed us differently. He could have crafted a sleepless humanity. He could have made us all Energizer bunnies who keep going and going and going. He could have structured our lives very differently. God could have designated one month a year as "sleep month" and commanded us to hibernate in order to stay awake for the rest of the year.

Or the Lord could have planned an entirely different system of nourishment for us. Why did He make us with a need for food every day? He could have orchestrated a weekly feast day on which we ate enough to last all week.

God could have made us more efficient. Imagine how much more we could get done if we didn't have to eat and sleep every day. Truck drivers could drive from North Carolina to California without stopping. Undergrads could pull all-nighters, cramming for finals without the slightest yawn. Surgeons could stay alert no matter how long they stood at the operating table. And think how long my sermons could be!

If *we* had been there at the foundation of the world, we probably would have made the creatures differently. We try to make things that have limitless energy. If IBM could design a laptop computer that never needed recharging, they'd control the market. If Chrysler could make a car that never needed refueling, they would take over the industry. And if Glaxo could synthesize a drug that guaranteed us the stamina of a marathon runner, we'd all empty our savings account for the injection.

But God made humans with distinct, daily needs. If we don't breathe every couple of seconds, we pass out. If we don't drink fluids every few hours, we dehydrate. If we don't eat, we starve. If we don't sleep, we get sick.

You can see it in every facet of our being. God did not make us to be self-sufficient creatures with boundless energy. He made us needy people who can't make it a day without refueling. Every breath, every swallow, every nap reminds us of our frailty. God made sure that His children could not go and go and go. He designed things so we would go...and stop, go...and stop, go...and stop.

He wove this pattern into the fabric of our being and then chiseled it in stone. He called it Sabbath—the fourth commandment.

"Remember the Sabbath day by keeping it holy. Six days you shall labor and do all your work, but the seventh day is a Sabbath to the LORD your God. On it you shall not do any work, neither you, nor your son or daughter, nor your man-servant or maidservant, nor your animals, nor the alien within your gates. For in six days the LORD made the heavens and the earth, the sea, and all that is in them, but he rested on the seventh day. Therefore the LORD blessed the Sabbath day and made it holy." (Exodus 20:8–11)

God meant it. He pronounced the most severe penalty for anyone who violated the fourth commandment: "Whoever does any work on the Sabbath day must be put to death" (Exodus 31:15). The Lord even declared that the earth itself needs sabbath.

> "When you enter the land I am going to give you, the land itself must observe a sabbath to the LORD. For six years sow your fields, and for six years prune your vineyards and gather their crops. But in the seventh year the land is to have a sabbath of rest, a sabbath to the LORD." (Leviticus 25:2–4)

Most Christians I know take the other nine commandments pretty seriously. For example, I don't know any Christians who murder on a regular basis. Yet I have almost no Christian friends who regularly observe the Sabbath. A lot of Christian ministers don't even take a day off each week.

Society actually applauds people who work constantly. Corporations promote employees who are willing to come early, stay late, and sneak in the office on weekends.

Ironically, the church may be the worst Sabbath offender. Our multitude of programs require a multitude of workers. Some people spend more time working at the church on Sunday than they do worshiping. I once knew a church treasurer who was so overworked on Sundays that he had to skip church to get some rest.

While there may be plenty of encouragement to keep the other commands, I hear little encouragement to keep the Sabbath. Many parishioners would quickly confront their pastor if he were caught lying from the pulpit or stealing from the offering. But when the pastor keeps no Sabbath, he gets subtle reinforcement. People say, "Pastor, you really ought to take a day off." But they're proud to tell others, "Our minister works so hard he doesn't even have time for a day off."

When someone actually practices Sabbath, the culture calls it laziness. How would you feel if your neighbor's lawn was overgrown, but he decided to lie in the hammock all day? When we finally do take a much-needed rest, we like to hide it. No adult wants to get caught napping. How do you act if the phone rings while you're taking an afternoon snooze or sleeping in on a Saturday morning?

In a way, it's strange that God even had to command a Sabbath. You would think that people would naturally be inclined to rest. In our sin, we are inclined toward slothfulness. In our selfishness, we normally relish the personal pleasures that time off brings. "Thou shalt not be lazy" didn't make the Ten Commandments. But the Sabbath law is mentioned over 130 times in the Scriptures.

God had to order us to observe Sabbath like a mother orders her child to take a nap. If we let him, I'm sure our two-year-old would skip his nap and stay up until he literally fell over. But a loving parent makes sure the child gets enough sleep.

The Lord is not content to let His children run themselves ragged. He knows how ornery His children get when they have no Sabbath. With no Sabbath to rest us and focus us, we become worse than any "napless wonder." God has seen how self-absorbed and prideful we become when we run constantly on our own agendas.

A soul that gets no Sabbath is like a stomach that gets no food, like a car that gets no new fuel, like lungs that get no breath, like a kid who gets no nap.

Sabbath, like all of God's laws, can be misconstrued and misused. The Pharisees did not observe Sabbath as refreshment for the soul but as a badge for their spiritual trophy cases.

The Sabbath is the one day we are free to accomplish nothing. How foolish to turn observing it into an accomplishment. How foolish to make the day of no work into a prideful work of righteousness.

For the Christian, Sabbath is not a curse meant to stifle but a means of grace to restore us. Sabbath is God's gracious permission for us to step out of the daily grind and accomplish nothing. One day a week God says you are to be totally unproductive. One day each week God wants you to completely goof off.

When you are successful at keeping one day totally

void of meaningful work, God will really bless you.

Sounds bizarre, doesn't it?

We are accustomed to being paid for what we produce. More work means more production means more income. The world judges us according to what we do. People ask, "What do you *do* for a living?" We even ask one another, "What did you *do* on vacation?"

Somewhere along the path to adulthood, we believed the lie that our self-worth is based on our level of accomplishment. We heard it so often that we finally accepted it. Our identity became confused with our performance. We became human *doings* and forgot we are human *beings*.

Sabbath is God's reminder that He loves you not for what you do but for who you are. Unlike worldly authorities, God does not bless you according to your performance. He sees your hard work, and He appreciates it. But He is inviting you regularly to set it all aside and just enjoy His presence.

Imagine a middle-aged man who decided to take up skiing. He planned a trip to a winter-wonderland resort on a distant mountain. He bought new skis, boots, poles, and some of the latest fashions. His first view of the slopes excited him. The snow sparkled. Skiers smiled as they swooshed back and forth across the hill.

Though he had never skied before, he was eager to

give it a try. How hard could it be? So the first-timer stumbled onto the lift and rode to the top of the mountain.

He started his descent. And, sure enough, it was easy. Just point the skis down the slope, aim them away from people and trees, and take off. That was his philosophy. And, amazingly, it worked.

He was not graceful. He scared more than a few other skiers. But, picking up speed as he went, the novice managed to race down the hill.

For a while, it was exhilarating. The wind whistled past his goggles. The powder flew around his boots. It was a thrilling ride. Until he thought about the bottom of the hill.

What would happen at the base of the mountain? Naively, he had just figured that the slope would gradually level out. He had imagined that his skis would naturally slow down over an extended flat area.

He was wrong. There was no gradual leveling of the slope. It came to an abrupt end. To his horror, the beginning skier saw nothing between him and the lodge except a row of skiers and a wooden fence. He hit them both.

On his way to the hospital, the ambitious skier wished he had taken a lesson on how to stop. And he discovered a skier's simple rule: The faster you go, the more you need to know about stopping.

Sabbath is God's solution to life's out-of-control crashes. God's command is simple and practical: Whatever you do in life, don't start until you know how to stop.

If you want to become like a child again, you'll have to learn to stop again. Stop being productive all the time. Stop earning money. Stop cleaning the house. Stop racing the clock. Stop *doing* something and just *be* somebody—a child of God.

In fact, maybe the best thing you could do is close this book. Shut your eyes. And take a little nap. Take a few moments to do nothing. The world will probably be here when you wake up. You're pretty important. But God doesn't need you to keep the world spinning. Sleep tight.

CHAPTER TWENTY-TWO

"I Want My Mommy"

Childlike Homesickness

*They admitted that they were aliens
and strangers on earth.*

HEBREWS 11:13

Due to a bout of temporary insanity, I once agreed to serve as a counselor for a cabin of third-grade boys at summer camp for a week. It will require at least an angelic visitation for me to ever become convinced that the Lord wants me to do it again. I was a Cub Scout dropout. I can only be considered an outdoorsman in that swimming pools and beaches are outdoors. The only outdoor trails I walk are on golf courses. The only knots I ever tie are accidental ones in my shoelaces, and I have a hard time distinguishing poison sumac from kudzu.

I should have been excited about the opportunity to have a whole week to share the love of Christ with these tender-hearted boys. Instead, my mission statement was more like "Get 'em here, keep 'em alive, get 'em outta here." I just wanted to keep them from stepping on a

236

snake or drowning under their capsized canoes. If I could send them home with no ticks in their hair and no Brown Recluse spider bites, who cared if they had learned archery or not? My main goal was to keep the boys within my sight and out of the infirmary.

So you can imagine my disappointment when my first night's sleep was interrupted by the sound of a moaning third-grader from a top bunk. At first I pulled my sleeping bag over my head, believing the dreaded noise would go away. Instead, it increased in both volume and frequency. I had no choice but to get up when the other boys woke up and began shining their flashlights toward the afflicted youngster. As I walked the lad toward the infirmary, he held his belly and talked of an upset stomach. My stomach hurt, too, as I considered the possibility of campwide food poisoning or, worse, a contagious intestinal virus.

The camp nurse was calm, however. She gently questioned the boy about his symptoms. "Can't sleep?… yes…Restless?…uh-huh…Empty feeling in your stomach?…I see." Obviously the nurse had seen this kind of thing before. Her last question confirmed her diagnosis. "Is this your first time away from home?"

The third-grade head nodded yes.

"Do you miss your mom and dad?"

A big tear rolled down my camper's face as he sputtered out the words, "Yes, ma'am."

"Homesickness," the nurse explained to me. "Happens

all the time. Especially with the young ones who've never been away from home before." She gave the boy some Pepto Bismol, a hug, and a promise that, if he wanted to, we'd call his parents the next morning.

There is only one real cure for homesickness, I discovered. Going home. But most children didn't have to resort to that. We managed to fill the summer-camp days with enough fun and activity that the children temporarily forgot how much they missed home. Give a kid enough hiking, leather crafting, and marshmallow roasting, and he'll manage without Mom for a while. Still, as much as they enjoyed camp, I never saw a little boy who wasn't excited about going home at the end of the week.

The homesick kids were picked on a bit. But all the children, if they were honest about it, could hardly wait for the sight of Mom and Dad's car at the camp gate.

After all, best friends are back home. The camp grub is nothing like Mom's home cooking. And the crowded cabin gets a little dirty and smelly after a while. And, as much as a kid hates to admit it, it's really nice to have Mom and Dad around. Phone calls and letters are nice, but they just don't compare to real hugs and kisses.

Homesickness is really nothing to be ashamed of. In fact, there'd be something wrong if a kid wanted to stay at camp forever.

It's hard to imagine, but one day my two-year-old will grow up enough to head off to summer camp. When he goes to camp for the first time, I hope he has a great adventure. I hope he doesn't get any ticks or spider bites, and I hope he learns archery. But I don't want him to like it so much that he forgets his mom and dad. As much as he might enjoy being away, I hope he always wants to come home.

I suppose homesickness is the only disease that parents would ever wish upon their child. It's the only sickness that can be a sign of a greater health.

I haven't walked another child to the Camp Grier infirmary since that visit twelve years ago. But I have walked beside dozens of grownups who have complained of the same symptoms. The symptoms are universal. The disease is no respecter of persons.

I remember the infirmary nurse when I attempt to make a pastoral assessment. "Can't sleep?...yes...Restless?....uh-huh...Empty feeling in your stomach?...I see." I probe a little further to confirm my diagnosis: "Do you ever feel like you're missing something?"

Sometimes the response is only a nod and a tear. Others express bewilderment while they rehearse their accomplishments. "I can't understand why I feel this way. I have everything I could want. A good mate. Fine children. A big house. A supportive church. A successful career. My life is so full, how could I feel so empty?"

Homesick for Heaven.

It's one disease God wants His children to have. He's

granted us freedom on earth. He's let us spend a brief
sojourn away from our Maker. But earth isn't home. It's
more like summer camp. God wants us to have a great
adventure, but He sure doesn't want us to get too comfortable here. We are "aliens and strangers" in the world.
We were made for more than this life, and God is not content for us to forget that simple truth.

So the Lord "set eternity in the hearts of men"
(Ecclesiastes 3:11). In fact, Paul implies that one of the
reasons God allows suffering is to keep us yearning for our
real home.

> The creation waits in eager expectation for the
> sons of God to be revealed. For the creation was
> subjected to frustration, not by its own choice, but
> by the will of the one who subjected it, in hope
> that the creation itself will be liberated from its
> bondage to decay and brought into the glorious
> freedom of the children of God. We know that the
> whole creation has been groaning as in the pains
> of childbirth right up to the present time. Not only
> so but we ourselves, who have the firstfruits of the
> Spirit, groan inwardly as we wait eagerly for our
> adoption as sons. (Romans 8:19–23)

Like the boy on the top bunk, don't you moan occasionally with a longing for eternity? Who can be satisfied

with this world? Even the best of moments are inadequate. Hearing my bride's "I do," our baby's first laugh, a sinner's first confession—as wonderful as these moments are, they serve only to prick my yearning for a place where all vows are kept, where babies are never stillborn, and where sin is banished. Heaven must be real because even the best of earth isn't enough.

We're all homesick. We all ache for more. Some just don't know what the ache is for.

So, like summer campers, we busy ourselves. Instead of canoeing, archery, and marshmallow roasting, we stay busy driving in traffic jams, shooting toward our career goals, and indulging in big buffets. The busyness dulls the pain of the inward ache.

It's not all bad, of course. We sometimes have meaningful work and endearing relationships. We get occasional, delicious tastes of the kingdom banquet to come. The clouds of sin sometimes depart long enough for a glimpse of heavenly light.

When you have enough tastes and enough glimpses, you begin to feel like Paul when he told the Philippians, "If I am to go on living in the body, this will mean fruitful labor for me. Yet what shall I choose? I do not know! I am torn between the two: I desire to depart and be with Christ, which is better by far" (Philippians 1:22–23).

But sadly, many get preoccupied with the world and make what Augustine called the worst mistake of all: "The only ultimate disaster that can befall us, I have come to realize, is to feel ourselves to be home on earth."[1]

Can you imagine a third-grade camper becoming so enamored with canoeing and archery lessons that he forgets he has a home awaiting his return? No child who has unconditional love, genuine affirmation, and consistent nurture at home would trade it all away for an endless marshmallow roast. But adults make such silly substitutes on a regular basis:

• Casual sex never satisfies the longing for heavenly love.
• Jack Daniels never quenches the thirst for celestial freedom.
• Mutual funds never profit like eternal riches.

Consider Max Lucado's word picture of homesickness:

Take a fish and place him on the beach. Watch his gills gasp and scales dry. Is he happy? No! How do you make him happy? Do you cover him with a mountain of cash? Do you get him a beach chair and sunglasses? Do you bring him a *Playfish* magazine and martini? Do you wardrobe him in double-breasted fins and people-skinned shoes? Of course not. Then how do you make him happy? You put him back in his element. You put him back in the water. He will never be happy on the beach simply because he was not made for the beach.[2]

When we get to Heaven we will be dazzled by a beauty that we could never have imagined. "No eye has seen, no ear has heard, no mind has conceived what God has prepared for those who love him" (1 Corinthians 2:9). We will marvel. But, at the same time, we will not be altogether surprised. Our entrance into eternity will not be as one stepping into a foreign, unfamiliar place. Instead, it will be more like arriving home after a long, tiring journey.

Jesus knew that his disciples would suffer from homesickness for Heaven. So He made them a clear promise. The promise stands for you and me as well. "In my Father's house are many rooms; if it were not so, I would have told you. I am going there to prepare a place for you. And if I go and prepare a place for you, I will come back and take you to be with me that you also may be where I am" (John 14:2–3).

If you're homesick, that's really what you need most— reassurance that you'll be back home soon. It sure helps you handle the problems and persecutions you face in an alien land just to be reminded that you've got a different home waiting for you.

The story is told of a faithful missionary sailing back to the United States after years of sacrificial ministry overseas. He wondered if anyone remembered him and hoped there would be people to greet him when his ship reached port.

Unknown to the missionary, there was a famous celebrity traveling aboard this same ship. A huge crowd of fans had gathered at the port to get a glimpse of the star's arrival.

At first, the missionary fantasized that perhaps the large crowd consisted of his supporting church members, gathered to welcome him home. As he exited the ship, though, the servant of God realized the crowd had come to see the celebrity. There was only one deacon there to greet the missionary and provide transportation from the port.

As they loaded the missionary's luggage into the car, the disappointed preacher said to the deacon, "It's kind of disheartening to see how much attention a movie star gets after a short trip out of the country. I've been away for years serving God, and there is no one to greet me when I get home."

The wise deacon responded, "But, sir, you're not home yet."

No earthly welcome for a famous star compares to the heavenly welcome for a glorified saint: "Our present sufferings are not worth comparing with the glory that will be revealed in us" (Romans 8:18).

We're all homesick.

A pastor once counseled a homeless man who claimed to be homesick. "But you have no home," the pastor declared. "How can you be homesick?"

The street dweller responded, "I'm homesick for the home I never had."[3]

If you've never met Christ, I'm sure you're looking for the home you've never had. The Spirit calls to you from eternity, "Do you want a home here?" All you need do is answer, "Yes, Lord. Prepare a place for me too."

If you've known the Lord but have wandered, you might be wondering if your room at home is still available. It is. As soon as you turn your heart toward home, the Father will see you from a distance and run to meet you.

If you are walking daily in God's grace, perhaps you're wondering if there's more. There sure is. You have a far better place prepared for you. You just haven't had the privilege of moving in there yet.

Jesus' invitation to childhood again may mean getting homesick for Heaven. But that's OK. Your Father won't leave you here forever. In the meantime, I suggest you call home often.

CHAPTER TWENTY-THREE

Labor Pains
Becoming a Child Again

Jesus declared, "I tell you the truth, no one can see the kingdom of God unless he is born again."

JOHN 3:3

I whistled softly as I stepped off the hospital elevator. I had no chemo patient's hand to hold that day. No "pre-op" prayers to pray. I had only one parishioner to visit, and though I had never met her, I knew for a fact that she was perfectly healthy. She had no disease. She was suffering no pain. She hadn't been in the world long enough to catch anything or break or bruise anything. Weighing in at around eight pounds, little Elizabeth wasn't yet a day old. Selfishly, I hurried to see the little miracle. I wanted to be among the first to say, "Welcome to the world." And so I whistled on my way to visit my newest parishioner.

But my little ditty was interrupted by a surprise sight. Walking past the waiting room, I noticed another member of our congregation. I learned that her daughter-in-law was currently in hard labor. As we talked, the expectant dad dropped by the waiting room to provide an update. Evidently his wife had been laboring all through the previous night. He had no idea how much longer it would be. She was slow in dilating. Labor might continue for hours.

He didn't say much else. There was no need. The whole scene was well painted across the first-time father's face. Plus, I remembered the feeling all too well. The awesome anticipation hidden behind the veil of uncertainty.

The few words of encouragement I offered were well received, but even I knew they carried a hollow echo. No matter how many obstetrician visits or ultrasounds, you really don't know that the baby is OK until she's in your hands, breathing, kicking, crying. With our prayers, the coach went back to his laboring wife, and I went on to visit a baby already born.

The new mom was sore but smiling. The new dad was unsure of himself but giddy. The baby was crying but perfect.

Staring at the tiny creature, I remembered our own son's birth. No other moment in life is comparable. A healthy baby arrives. A lifetime of possibility begins. How soon the new mother forgets the anguish of labor. How quickly the father dismisses his earlier fears.

Following those few minutes of wonder, I made my way back to the elevator. As I passed by the waiting room, the expectant grandma smiled at me nervously. With one more hug and a silent prayer, I left the grandmother waiting, the father coaching, and the mother laboring.

Thankfully, the second baby was born later that day. He, too, was healthy and beautiful.

But the morning's scene lingered in my mind. The babies could hardly have been closer. Less than a day apart. But in those moments of my hospital visit, the two infants could not have seemed more distant. The two babies would arrive on planet Earth within twelve hours of each other, but for a few indescribable moments those parents felt they lived in totally different worlds.

The chasm seems vast between a baby in a mother's womb and a baby in a mother's arms. Yet, they are remarkably close. They are only a birth and a blinking apart. The baby in the womb and the baby in the world is the same marvelous creature. But once in the world, the infant breathes new air, sees new light, feels a new embrace.

Does childhood seem insurmountably distant to you? It is not. A childlike life is remarkably close. New, celestial air is as close as your next breath. Bright, heavenly light is as close as your next blink. Your Father's embrace is as close as your next tear.

But there's only one way to become a child again— birth.

"You *must* be born again," Jesus said (John 3:7). No exceptions. It's not so much a law as it is a fact.

There is only one way onto planet Earth. You must be born. Do you know anyone who wasn't born? You might have been plucked out by Cesarean section or pulled out by forceps, but you were born. You might have been the product of artificial insemination or uterine implant, but you came into the world like everyone else. Every one of us once lived in a cramped, dark place where we breathed water and were fed through a tube. If you are here, we all know how you got here. You must be born in order to breathe Earth's air or to feel Earth's clay. No exceptions.

And when I say, "You must be born in order to live on Earth," I'm not prescribing a duty. I'm just stating a fact.

When Jesus told Nicodemus that "no one can see the kingdom of God unless he is born again" (John 3:3), the Lord was not heaping another duty on the inquisitive Pharisee. He was just declaring a truth.

It is the same truth that Jesus taught his curious disciples when they asked the question that prompted me to write this book: "Who is the greatest in the kingdom of heaven?"

"I tell you the truth, unless you change and become like little children, you will never enter the kingdom of heaven" (Matthew 18:3). It's not another rule to keep or a duty to perform. It's just a fact. It's an invitation.

And it's wonderful news.

For if Jesus said you *must* become like a little child, it means you *can*. Jesus never issues impossible decrees. He never prescribes unattainable cures.

Don't miss the symbol that Jesus painted for

Nicodemus. An old man becoming a tiny baby. Imagine it. Wrinkled skin, blotched by years of hot Judean sun and weathered by arid, mideastern winds, becoming soft, pink, and unblemished. Don't let the familiarity of the verse blur the incredible contrast. "Be born again." Old arteries inwardly rusted with years of unhealthy appetite replaced with unscarred vessels flowing with untainted blood. Sagging muscles, brittle bones, and stiff joints transformed into the nimble, elastic anatomy of a toddler.

That's how dramatic the change is that Jesus offers. Our coarse, protective exteriors, weathered with years of the world's abrasion, really can become soft and receptive again. Our thoughts, clogged with years of disappointment and bitterness, can flow freely, purely again. Our stiff souls, tightened by years of pride and self-will, can become supple again.

The chance at childhood again is real. Jesus wasn't just painting interesting word pictures, He was inviting Nicodemus into the kingdom. Now, He's inviting you.

Here's even better news.

The invitation to childhood again is wonderful because your birth, the most important moment of your earthly life, was not your own accomplishment. Your birth was your greatest victory, but you had nothing to do with achieving it. You didn't labor; your mother did. You didn't deliver yourself into the world; your doctor did. You didn't pay the hospital bill; your father did.

It was your greatest moment—your most important moment—your most celebrated moment. And you were just there for the ride.

That's the way birth is. It's not something that you do. It's something that happens to you.

Jesus is not sitting nervously in some heavenly waiting room hoping that you make it into the kingdom safely. He made you from eternity. He labored for you on the cross. He's ready to deliver you. He'll do it all. Only one thing is required of you.

You must give up the womb.

The first nine months of your life were surely the most comfortable months you ever spent. You floated carelessly in your one-room world. Everything was soft. It was always warm. No work was required. You didn't even have to chew.

Birth, on the other hand, is messy business. Entering the world is risky. It's definitely softer and cozier in the womb.

But it's quite cramped in a mother's uterus. There's no way to stretch out. No way to grow. It would have been more comfortable to stay in the warm womb, but consider what you would have missed. You would never have felt your mother's kiss or seen your father's smile. You would never have clapped your hands or marched in a parade. You would never have known the joy of meeting a new friend or felt the pleasure of holding a mate's hand.

Becoming a child again means letting go of the womb of pride that we have so carefully constructed on the path to adulthood. It's scary because it means letting go of almost everything we've been taught.

When your life is phony, childlike candor is frightening. When your self-worth is built upon personal success, childlike failure seems horrifying. When your safety net is sameness, childlike imagination is unsettling. When your strength is sophistication, childlike astonishment seems weak.

If leaving the womb of the world for the life of the kingdom feels scary, let me leave you with the best news of all. Jesus' chance at childhood again is not an invitation to become an orphan. It is an offer to become His brother. You'll never find a better big brother. It is an opportunity to sit in His Father's lap. You'll never find a bigger lap. It is a chance to play in the royal courtyard. You'll never find a finer playground.

Jesus is not offering an invitation to become just any child. He's offering an invitation to become God's child. And being God's child carries incredible privileges.

God loves all of creation. But His affection is irretrievably set upon His own children.

I love all children. We support two overseas children, and I'd like to support fifty more. If you have children, I'm sure they are precious and beautiful. But do I care about your children like I care for my own little boy? Honestly?

No way. I'm sure your children are cute, but I'm not planning on setting up a college fund for your kids until I get one going for mine.

I needn't be ashamed to say I hold more affection for my own child than I do for yours. After all, I'm his father.

And God isn't ashamed to tell of His undying affection for His own children: "Now if we are children, then we are heirs—heirs of God and co-heirs with Christ" (Romans 8:17). He is unashamed to tell His children how wide, how long, how deep, how high is His love for us. He is unembarrassed to announce the lavish plans He has for us.

My wife cares for Bennett most of the day and most days. But ready for relief, and eager for me to spend time with our boy, Anne grants me the privilege of putting Bennett to bed almost every night. We read some, giggle some, pray some, and sing some. But as time to say good night draws near, I always sing the same little song.

It's not particularly poetic or clever. Its melody is not particularly memorable. But I've sung it to Bennett from the earliest days of his infancy. And now, if I don't volunteer the song, my boy will often request it: "Daddy, sing 'Baby Boy.'" And so I sing:

> You are my baby boy.
> You are my baby boy.
> And your father really loves you,
> Oh, how much he loves you.

Never will he leave you,
Never will he deceive you.
And always, always, he will believe in you,
For you are, and always will be, my baby boy.

And as I sing and gently squeeze that quiet toddler in my arms every night, I feel strangely embraced as well. I realize that I'm not so much singing as being sung to. I hear it so clearly. Not audibly, but inwardly. Quietly the Spirit sings, "Your Father really loves you. Oh, how much He loves you." Gently He rocks my soul and reassures, "Never will He leave you. Never will He deceive you. Always He will believe in you."

And so most of my days end with one simple, nourishing decision. I hope you'll make it yours too. "There's nothing I'd rather be than God's baby boy."

A Father's Good Night

Good night, little boy.

No more stories tonight. No…that was the last one.
I know you don't want to go to bed. But little boys need sleep.

Your boo boo hurts?
OK. I'll kiss it. Come close to Daddy.

Close now, little eyes.
Who knows what wonders you might dream up? New sights await you tomorrow.

Quiet down, little hands.

Tomorrow you'll fingerpaint a masterpiece. We'll hang it on the refrigerator.

Calm yourselves, giddy arms.

Goliath is already down. You can tumble more giants tomorrow.

Stop scurrying, little legs.

There are plenty of trails for hiking tomorrow's woods.

Hush, silly voice.

You can squeal with delight when you splash in the sprinkler tomorrow.

Rest peacefully, beating heart.

I'll keep watch by night. No evil can overtake you without going through me first.

Sleep well, slumbering boy. Night-night. I love you.

Lord, bless my sleeping son. Don't let him change too much. Keep him in Bible stories and hugs and kisses. Keep that sparkle in his eyes and creativity in his fingers. Don't let his arms stop swinging or his legs stop marching. Keep the squeal of freedom in his voice and the splash of adventure in his soul. And when he is grown, let him still sleep like a baby.

I pray for my son, but perhaps he should pray for me.

Pray for my life. Why has the bed, once such a foe, become such a friend?

Pray for my hurts. Who'll kiss my wounded heart?

Pray for my vision. Another day has come and gone. Is this all there is, Lord?

Pray for my hands. What's left to create?

Pray for my arms. Lord, my Goliath is still standing …and I'm out of smooth stones.

Pray for my legs. What path are they on? Or is this a treadmill I'm walking?

Pray for my voice. When did it last squeal with delight? Where has my giggle gone?

Pray for my peace. I'm so tired…tomorrow's a tough day…why can't I sleep?

Oh Lord, my boy wants to be like me. But oh, how I want to be like him.

Good night, child of God. I'll make you like him.

I'll bless your life. Here, drink this living water.

I'll bless your brokenness. Here, let My Comforter kiss your heart.

I'll bless your eyes. You can't imagine what's in store tomorrow.

I'll bless your hands. Tomorrow's masterpiece will hang on Heaven's gates.

I'll bless your arms. You are more than a conqueror in Christ.

I'll bless your legs. You've got a race to finish—and the prize awaits.

I'll bless your voice. Go ahead and shout "Hallelujah!" Doesn't that tickle?

I'll bless your heart. My peace I give you, not like the world's. Real peace.

Sleep well. I'll keep watch by night. No one can get to you without going through Me first. Sleep well, little child of God. Freedom and wonder await.

"I tell you the truth,
unless you change and become like little children,
you will never enter the kingdom of Heaven."

Notes

CHAPTER 7

1. Albert M. Wells Jr., *Inspiring Quotations: Contemporary and Classical* (Nashville: Thomas Nelson, 1988), p. 220.

CHAPTER 9

1. Rudolph Otto, *The Idea of the Holy* (Oxford: Oxford University Press, 1950), pp. 12–13.

2. All the sideshows mentioned are actual advertisements as quoted in *Durham Herald-Sun*.

CHAPTER 10

1. *USA Today*, 11 March 1996.

2. Thanks to the Rev. Stanley Bennett for this insight shared in late-night conversations.

CHAPTER 12

1. Lee Bryan donated his disclosure to Duke University Medical Center in 1971. The idea was then developed using other research and later patented.

2. Oswald Chambers, *My Utmost for His Highest* (1935; reprint, Westwood, N.J.: Barbour and Company, Inc., 1963), p. 42.

3. James Hewitt, ed., *Illustrations Unlimited* (Wheaton: Tyndale House Publishers, 1989), pp. 389–90.

4. See Richard Foster's *Celebration of Discipline* (1978; rev. ed. San Francisco: Harper and Row Publishers, Inc., 1988), p. 25, for his insightful description of a "sanctified imagination."

CHAPTER 17

1. Ruth Hulbert Hamilton, *Meditations for the Expectant Mother,* ed. Helen Good Brenneman (Scottdale, Pa.: Herald Press, 1985), p. 48.

CHAPTER 19

1. Sue Bender, *Plain and Simple: A Woman's Journey to the Amish* (Harper San Francisco, 1991), p. 5.

2. Ibid., p. 48.

3. Ibid., p. 64.

CHAPTER 20

1. James Dobson, *Dare to Discipline* (Wheaton: Tyndale House Publishers, 1970), p. 44.

CHAPTER 22

1. Augustine, *Confessions*, quoted by Max Lucado in *When God Whispers Your Name* (Dallas: Word Publishing, 1994), p. 172.

2. Lucado, *When God Whispers Your Name*, p. 173.

3. Told by the Rev. Stanley Bennett.